Forsaken Gospel

*How Denominational Christianity
Lost the Way*

Bronwyn Cochran Randel

ISBN 979-8-88943-097-1 (paperback)
ISBN 979-8-88943-098-8 (digital)

Copyright © 2024 by Bronwyn Cochran Randel

All rights reserved. No part of this publication may be reproduced, distributed, or transmitted in any form or by any means, including photocopying, recording, or other electronic or mechanical methods without the prior written permission of the publisher. For permission requests, solicit the publisher via the address below.

Christian Faith Publishing
832 Park Avenue
Meadville, PA 16335
www.christianfaithpublishing.com

All biblical citations were taken from the New International Version of the Holy Bible unless otherwise indicated.

Cover art used by permission Cathryn C. Olympiadis, copyright 2023

Printed in the United States of America

To the Upper Room class,
who were instrumental in the creation of this manuscript.

For the word of God is living and active. Sharper than any double-edged sword, it penetrates even to dividing soul and spirit, joints and marrow; it judges the thoughts and attitudes of the heart.
—Hebrews 4:12

CONTENTS

Preface xi
Introduction xv

Chapter 1   Introduction: The Arrival 1
Chapter 2   Forsaken Bible 10
Chapter 3   Forsaken God 18
Chapter 4   Forsaken Man 33
Chapter 5   Forsaken Family 39
Chapter 6   Forgotten Enemy 50
Chapter 7   Forsaken Salvation 58
Chapter 8   Forsaken Church 74
Chapter 9   Forsaken Redeemer 83
Chapter 10   Ears to Hear: Metaphorical Consistency 88
Chapter 11   Forsaken Stars 106
Chapter 12   Conclusion: Satan's Haymaker and the Real
             Conspiracy 120
Appendix 1 Mazzaroth 135
Appendix 2 Transposition, C.S. Lewis 177
Appendix 3 Translation Clarification 189

PREFACE

This book is not a Bible study or a personal devotional, but I sincerely hope that you do as the noble Bereans did when they heard the Apostle Paul's teaching: they studied the scriptures for themselves to see if such things were true. Thanks to the internet, it has never been easier to compare Bible translations and find one that suits you. If you haven't already done so, find one now so that you can read the Bible for yourself, mainly just to see what it actually says. Avoid paraphrased versions; they are someone's subjective interpretation that does not always adhere to the original text. On the other hand, a translation preserves the metaphorical consistency that is demonstrated throughout the complete text and confirms its divine authority.

    The goal is to learn to hear what God is saying to you, with no middleman or tutor except the Holy Spirit. That is God's desire. In fact, that's why He created you, that you would be a partaker of His divine nature (that phrase comes from the Apostle Peter), always in communion with Him as His own precious child. Nobody should be dependent on somebody else's Bible reading in order to hear what their Father is saying.

Preface

Some basic obstacles complicate our ability to communicate. Human language has been shape-shifting nonstop ever since we discovered we could say "yes" and "no," precipitating that horrible incident in the garden of Eden when Adam and Eve chose to disobey God's only rule. Now that we're in the digital age, language shifting is even more hectic. New words are being conceived, gestated, and delivered into public usage at an ever-increasing rate. The world has never been smaller, and when human groups interact, languages meld, commandeer useful terms from each other, and produce unexpected hybrids.

Every generation makes its mark on the language as well. Language influences history, and history influences language. Advances in technology necessitate adaptations in the use of language, from vocabulary (Who knew emojis would become so important?) to syntax and punctuation. The meaning of long-standing familiar terms can mutate, resulting in situations in which a particular expression means something totally different to your child than it does to you.

Sadly, people use language at least as much to mislead as to inform. Political, social, and advertising campaigns bank on the fact that their slogans will influence behavior without actually conveying any meaning. All of us have, at one time or another, witnessed (or taken part in) heated exchanges in which the participants were not even talking about the same thing. The most serious problem, though, is that we are adept at using language to deceive ourselves.

Biblical or religious vocabulary is especially troublesome, as you can imagine. Friendly discussions about the Bible, Christianity, or the church are tricky because even the term *Christian* might have a different meaning for one person in the conversation than it does for the others. Biblical expressions shift meaning over time in the same way other words do; terms like *church, religion, faith,* and *Christian* carry connotations now that bear almost no resemblance to the original biblical usage and can mean vastly different things to people from different communities. Concepts that once were considered common knowledge, like *sin, judgment, shame,* and *hell,* have been swept under the rug, where they will, some hope, not attract much attention. Well-educated and influential public leaders, although identifying themselves as Christian, welcome these developments. Faithful American churchgoers, comfortable with the label "good Christian," are often skillful with religious jargon while remaining ignorant of the Bible's plainly written message.

What's more, ancient history and archaeology continue to inspire books, articles, documentaries, blogs, and podcasts that do not always demonstrate intellectual integrity. Some of the creators of these texts might not even know there is such a thing. Google, Reddit, YouTube, and Wikipedia (et al.) put a stupefying amount of information on any topic literally at your fingertips, but internet resources can be dangerous, especially for biblical or religious topics; they attract more than their fair share of charlatans (and crackpots). These sites can sometimes provide useful information, but you need to keep an open mind and maintain your own intellectual integrity.

Mutual understanding is the basis of communication, and the message mankind needs most of all is the good news, that, to our shame, we American Christians—in spite of unhindered access to the Bible—have dropped by the wayside, forsaken, and left for dead. Returning to the original narrative is a good start for clarifying the Bible's message. No cherry-picking to find particular verses that support your own cherished convictions or telling God beforehand what you want to know; just reading to learn what He is saying.

This has nothing to do with political action, or social justice, or self-actualization. It's to do with what the Book says. And to emphasize again: **Nobody should be dependent on somebody else's Bible reading.** God is your heavenly Father, and He wants to speak with you just as much as with anyone else. He loves you.

Let me give you a heads up:

Each section in this book addresses a biblical concept that, although once intrinsic to Christianity and common knowledge in American culture, is now considered irrelevant or unacceptable and has therefore been forsaken. In twenty-first-century lingo, the term would be ~~cancelled~~ canceled. (*I just this minute learned that the double l "cancelled" is more acceptable in British English, while the single l "canceled" is more American. Both are acceptable.*)

Preface

Biblical vocabulary, topics, concepts, imagery, and themes are so interrelated that pulling a single strand away from its neighbors is impossible. No matter where you start, you will unavoidably meet issues insisting that you choose a direction, and whichever way you go, what you find will seem redundant and will eventually lead you back to where you started. It's like a verbal fractal, continually developing like mad, but never changing. Like quantum physics, God's Word is paradoxical. In *Forsaken Gospel*, you might find material in one place that you think would fit better in a different section, and you would not be wrong. For that reason, the chapters do not necessarily need to be read in the order they appear, and some material appears more than once.

INTRODUCTION

The historical epoch between the last biblical prophet Malachi and the appearance of John the Baptist, known as the 400 Silent Years, witnessed the ascent of the Greek Empire that had been fueled by Alexander the Great's defeat of the Persians. King Cyrus of Persia during this time had authorized the Hebrew exiles to return to Jerusalem and begin rebuilding the temple.

Distinguished by thinkers such as Plato, Aristotle, and the elusive Socrates, this era was characterized by an unprecedented interest in philosophical issues such as the nature of reality, the definition of truth, and the meaning of life. Interestingly, the Greek term for "word," *logos,* was appropriated by philosophers during this time to signify the concept of an underlying reality that sustains everything else; so when the Apostle John wrote, "The word (*logos*) became flesh and dwelt among us," his contemporaries knew exactly what he meant.

While advancing toward Jerusalem, Alexander had a dream in which he saw a group of men in black robes standing in the way, and he knew that he needed to listen to them. As he neared the city, a group of rabbis, wearing black robes and carrying a scroll, came out to beg him not to destroy their ancient capital, which they had so recently regained. They opened the scroll to the second chapter in the book of Daniel, showed Alexander Nebuchadnezzar's dream of the enormous statue, and explained how that prophecy applied to him. (This event is recorded in several ancient texts, and not all agree in every detail.)

Alexander not only did not sack the city but recruited seventy rabbis to come to the library in Alexandria, Egypt, to produce a Greek translation of the Hebrew Bible, which thereafter became known as the Septuagint. Alexander's early death opened the way for Rome to dominate the entire Mediterranean world, making historic progress in military science, engineering, and civic amenities, constructing roads, aqueducts, and huge venues for popular entertainment. Human society was fertile soil for the message of the gospel.

CHAPTER 1

Introduction
The Arrival

The virgin shall conceive and bear a son, and will call him Emmanuel.
—Isa. 7:14

A couple of millenia ago, give or take a decade or two, a baby was born in a town called Bethlehem, located in the tiny nation of Judea. Situated on the easternmost shore of the Mediterranean Sea, it was being crushed under the boot of the Roman Empire. At this particular point in time, God had sent no prophets to minister to the Hebrews for about four hundred years, but the oppressed nation was still clinging to their Bible's promises of the Anointed One (in the Greek language, Christ; in Hebrew, Messiah) who would rescue them and restore their independence.

The extraordinary birth and the astonishing events that accompanied it were well-documented by first-person eyewitnesses at the time. A young woman delivered her firstborn, a son, in a stable,

Introduction: The Arrival

which quite possibly was located directly underneath the inn's first floor. She was attended only by her betrothed husband, who knew the baby was not his.

These circumstances are not a heartwarming myth or an inspirational legend. We don't know if Joseph had ever participated in the delivery of a human infant before, but he was a carpenter, so he would have at least carried a sharp knife. The animals' bodies and breath would have kept the stable warm, and fresh, sweet-smelling hay would have provided clean bedding. In fact, it might have been more private, quieter, and more comfortable than the inn, which was packed to overflowing.

Mary, the mother, had brought swaddling clothes for the baby. She had been visited by the angel Gabriel some months earlier, who told her that she was going to become pregnant—never mind that she was a virgin—and that her male child would be the Son of God. An angel had also visited her intended husband, Joseph, in a dream and assured him that he shouldn't be afraid to take her home as his wife, because her pregnancy was from the Holy Spirit. (It is no coincidence that the first constellation in the *Mazzaroth*, Virgo, is a virgin carrying a seed and a branch. More about that later.)

At about the same time, Mary's elderly and childless cousin Elizabeth had also miraculously become pregnant. Her aged husband, Zechariah, a priest ministering in the temple, had been appointed that year to perform the required annual service in the holy of holies. While behind the veil, he experienced a supernatural visitation as well. The angel, once again identified as Gabriel, told Zechariah that his wife—though she was past childbearing age and had always been barren anyway—would give birth to a prophet who would make the people ready for the Lord. The angel told Zechariah to name the child John.

Because Zechariah didn't believe it immediately, Gabriel (who apparently was not a beautiful female with golden curls and snowy wings, clad in a shimmering toga and emanating peace and mercy as popular culture would have it; these are the same folks who can't believe in the "God of the Old Testament.") struck Zechariah dumb until the child was born. At least Zechariah didn't fall to the ground as if dead. Old Testament angels sometimes had that effect on people. When Gabriel visited Daniel, the prophet was totally overwhelmed, rendered unconscious, and remained physically ill for weeks afterward.

When Mary visited Elizabeth during her pregnancy, the moment they saw each other, the baby in Elizabeth's womb (John the Baptist) recognized the baby in Mary's womb (Jesus, the Messiah) inspiring some of the most beautiful and profound poetry ever recorded. The "Ave Maria," recorded in the Gospel of Luke, chapter 1, remains a significant component of the Catholic faith, and the song by Franz Schubert is not only a staple of religious Christmas celebrations but even now is a familiar inclusion in classical voice performances.

Shortly after the only begotten Son of God was born in the stable, some shepherds arrived with an astounding report of innumerable angels in the sky celebrating the coming of the Messiah, and who told them where to find Him—in a stable. Snuggled down in an animal's feeding trough.

SERIOUSLY? Are you KIDDING? Who devised THIS myth?

Herod the Great, Judea's king at the time, is historically notable because of his restoration of the Second Temple in Jerusalem. A short time after the birth in the stable, a group of learned men, who we're told had traveled a long way from the East, informed Herod that they had seen the star that signaled the arrival of the King of the Jews, and they had come to worship Him.

Who were <u>they</u>? Where did they come from? How did they know about the Messiah? Where did they learn to read the stars? There are no insignificant details in the Bible, and all of the explanations are included in the text. Somewhere. (Proverbs 25:2 states that it is the glory of God to conceal a matter, and the glory of kings to search it out.)

Aside from the shepherds and the wise men, no one else seems to have been aware of anything unusual in the sky at the time. Herod certainly wasn't. As a result of the alarming news, he ordered the massacre of every boy in Bethlehem aged two and under, which he hoped would keep his throne, supported by Rome, unchallenged. However, Joseph had already escaped with his family into Egypt,

Introduction: The Arrival

having been warned in a second dream that Herod wanted to kill the baby.

Some time later, another dream notified Joseph that Herod had died, so he brought Mary and Jesus back and settled in Nazareth, in Galilee. These events absolutely create a truly dramatic narrative, in spite of the necessary omission of many wonderful details, so that this book could be finished at some point before I lay this body down. As John states:

> *Jesus did many other things as well. If every one of them were written down, I suppose that even the whole world would not have room for the books that would be written.* (John 21:25)

Throughout history, until the arrival of the Messiah, important events all over the world were usually referenced to a known ruler or a cataclysm of some sort, as in Isaiah's statement, "In the year King Uzziah died..." or perhaps something like "in the summer before the earthquake." The ancient Chinese calendar restarted at year one whenever a new dynasty took power, and the numbering of years was continuing to be researched, debated, and retroactively adapted well into the twentieth century.

Unlike scriptures of other faiths, the Bible always documents the time and place of each incident, in addition to the people involved. Not like a myth at all. In fact, the second chapter of Luke opens with "the five *W*'s," exactly as student journalists learn: who, what, when, where, why.

> *In those days Caesar Augustus issued a decree that a census should be taken of the entire Roman world. This was the first census that took place while Quirinius was governor of Syria. And everyone went to their own town to register. So Joseph also went up from the town of Nazareth in Galilee to Judea, to Bethlehem the town of David, because he belonged to the house and line of David.* (Luke 2:1–4)

Luke is obviously taking care to put together a valid historical record. The information he includes can be checked against contemporaneous sources to be verified or repudiated.

The first universal standardized calendar was being developed at this point in history; Julius Caesar was one of those who came up with a workable option. Interestingly, the use of a seven-day week was already widespread. The effect of the Messiah's arrival at this particular confluence of events resulted in the acceptance of the notations "BC" (Before Christ) and "AD" (Anno Domini, the year of the Lord) to differentiate between years preceding a known point—that extraordinary birth in the stable—and years following it. Until recently (*World Almanac* converted in 2007) this system was found to be convenient for just about everyone.

Evidently, the birth in the stable had become such an odious stench to twenty-first-century emerging powers-that-want-to-be it was deemed inappropriate for its position as an unavoidable benchmark and was therefore *canceled*. BC became BCE (Before Common Era), and AD became CE (Common Era). This way, non-Christians won't feel uncomfortable when they come across the usage of these calendar abbreviations.

Was the use of BC and AD akin to allowing religion to influence official government business? The separation of church and state could be described, without irony, as *gospel* (good news) to some notable figures in the American political arena. Christian evangelism has been branded as an instigator of nineteenth-century colonialism, which led to the devastation of social and cultural networks around the globe, right? Those initials are considered by some to be nothing less than weapons of an oppressive system that needed to be eliminated. Nevertheless, the pivotal point in human history remains the birth in the stable.

Note:

Jews have been using their own sophisticated astral/solar/lunar calendar since the time of Moses, about 1600 ~~BC~~ BCE. Each year is organized around holy days that God commanded them to observe, beginning with Passover, so that they would remember the miracles

Introduction: The Arrival

He had performed for them and keep watching for the Messiah. Maimonides, an influential twelfth century rabbi, calculated that the Hebrew exodus from Egypt took place 2,448 years after the creation of the world, which means that, according to him, Jesus of Nazareth would have been born in or about the year 3760. It is now year 5782 on the Hebrew calendar, 2022 for others. But wait…

Okay, all that is definitely noteworthy. But what is *staggering* is that almost every detail in the New Testament accounts of the nativity is the fulfillment of at least one, sometimes more, specific prophecies found in the Hebrew Bible, the Original Testament. This holds true for the entire record of His conception, birth, life, death, resurrection, and ascension, followed by the outpouring of the Holy Spirit and the birth of the church.

For example, the Bible associates three locations with the arrival of the Messiah: Bethlehem, Egypt, and Nazareth. Jesus of Nazareth fulfills them all.

> *But you, Bethlehem Ephrathah, though you are small among the clans of Judah, out of you will come for me one who will be ruler over Israel, whose origins are from of old, from ancient times.* (Mic. 5:2)
>
> *Out of Egypt I have called my son.* (Hosea 11:1)
>
> *A shoot will come up from the stump of Jesse; from his roots a Branch will bear fruit.* (Isa. 11:1)

The word translated branch is *netzer*, which is the base of the place name Nazareth. Branch is a significant symbol regularly used in the Bible, as well as in the *Mazzaroth*, to denote the Messiah. (More about this elsewhere.)

Throughout the New Testament, the Apostle Paul, Apollos, and others are continuously described as "using the scriptures" to prove that Jesus of Nazareth is the Messiah, the Anointed One promised by God in ages past. Which scriptures would they have been using? Of course, it must have been the Hebrew Bible, which Christians somewhat naïvely call the Old Testament. ("Original Testament" is more accurate.) The New Testament was only just in the process of being written. Jesus had even told the Pharisees to their faces that the scriptures they expected to bring them eternal life were actually written about Him. Here are a couple of examples:

– The Messiah would be born of a virgin:

In *Genesis* 3, God tells the serpent that the seed of the woman would crush his head. This is the protoevangelium, the first mention of the gospel, the good news, about the Messiah's defeat of Satan. This passage somewhat undermines accusations of biblical misogyny. Later, about 740 BC, Isaiah wrote:

> *Therefore the Lord himself will give you a sign: The virgin will conceive and give birth to a son, and will call him Immanuel.* (Isa. 7:14)

– Innocent children would be massacred:

Matthew refers to a passage from *Jeremiah* 31, written about six hundred years previously:

> *"A voice is heard in Ramah, weeping and great mourning, Rachel weeping for her children and refusing to be comforted, because they are no more."* (Matt. 2:18)

The second chapter of *Exodus* records Pharoah's attempts in the sixteenth century BC to have all male Hebrew children killed at birth. (Repeated prophetic patterns are called ensamples.)

Here's a passage from *Zechariah*, written about 520 BC:

> *Rejoice greatly, Daughter Zion! Shout, Daughter Jerusalem! See, your king comes to you, righteous*

Introduction: The Arrival

and victorious, lowly and riding on a donkey, on a colt, the foal of a donkey. (Zech. 9:9)

The once familiar triumphal entry is almost always depicted in illustrated Bibles or Bible story books:

Jesus found a young donkey and sat on it, as it is written: "Do not be afraid, Daughter Zion! See, your king is coming, Seated on a donkey's colt." At first his disciples did not understand all this. Only after Jesus was glorified did they realize that these things had been written about Him and that these things had been done to Him. (John 12:14–16)

Some thirty-three years after His birth in the stable, the only begotten Son of God submitted Himself to the worst of mankind's brutality, tortured until He was no longer recognizable, then hung from a stake by nails driven through His hands until he was dead. He gave up His own blood and His own life, Himself receiving the vengeance that was necessary to resolve the sin of mankind.

When they had executed Him, they divided up His clothes by casting lots. (Matt. 27:35)

Would the Roman soldiers gambling for His clothes have known they were fulfilling a prophecy more than one thousand years old? It's found in *Psalm* 22, written by the second Hebrew king, David:

Dogs surround me, a pack of villains encircles me; they pierce my hands and my feet. All my bones are on display; people stare and gloat over me. They divide my clothes among them and cast lots for my garment. (Ps. 22:16–18)

Prophecies found in the Hebrew Bible—the Original Testament—could not have been written less than five hundred years before the baby was born in the stable. In fact, some would have been written more than 1000, or even 1500, years earlier, but the New Testament is meaningless without the ancient Hebrew Scriptures. We know Jesus is the Messiah because He fulfilled the Bible's prophecies; we know that the Bible is God's Word because its prophecies have been, and are still being, fulfilled. The Messiah, Jesus of Nazareth, the Lord Jesus Christ, the only begotten Son of God, in His life among us at the merging of Greek and Roman culture, fulfilled hundreds of prophetic details found in the Bible. This is not conjecture. **Hundreds.**

CHAPTER 2
Forsaken Bible

For the word of God is living and active. Sharper than any double-edged sword, it penetrates even to dividing soul and spirit, joints and marrow; it judges the thoughts and attitudes of the heart.
—Heb. 4:12

The Bible's content can be characterized as prophecies and promises within a historical context spanning more than two thousand years. The Bible is the archetype of archetypes, unique in human literature. Its sixty-six separate books represent widely divergent styles and genres, everything from history to suspense, drama to autobiography and biography, personal letters and legal documents, employing both prose and poetry (no fiction, though). The Bible includes works that exemplify the highest standard of literary excellence and features at least thirty-five different writers from a cross section of social and cultural spheres. None of this is disputed. The fact that this book even exists is miraculous.

In spite of the diversity of its multiple writers, each biblical topic, or strand, or concept, is inextricably interwoven with all the others. Once begun, a search can open into a variety of directions, and each of those opens up a new array of opportunities, and so on and so forth—it's like fractal permutations into infinity. It is, in fact, only one thread, folded, twisted, wound around itself, doubling back, one continuous looping thread, creating a tapestry that ultimately conveys only one idea: God created you, and He loves you beyond comprehension.

Many writers but one Author. The Bible is the written Word of God, the standard of truth against which everything else is measured. (An interesting departure from common practice is that, according to Genesis, the twenty-four-hour day is measured from sunset to sunset, instead of the more obvious sunrise to sunrise. A small detail, but a hint that the assertions of this book cannot be fully explained by human ingenuity.) The book of *Genesis* is sufficient within itself to explain everything about the world: why the universe operates the way it does, why nature functions the way it does, why human beings think and behave as we do, and why nations prosper or decline.

Literacy is one of the factors that demonstrate humankind's exclusive position of "created in the image of God." The gift of literacy enables people to receive God's revelation of Himself, not only through the material universe that He provided as our habitat but also through the written Word.

A phonetic alphabet assigns sounds, rather than meaning, to each written symbol. The use of a phonetic alphabet, rather than a symbolic or hieroglyphic one, makes literacy accessible for common people because it's inexpensive and easy to learn. Before phonics, rulers and merchants required the service of a specially educated class of scribes, or clerks, to keep track of historical events, financial records, and other important information.

Many scholars believe that the Phoenicians got the idea of a sound-based alphabet from a nomadic tribe in the Sinai desert who had been heavily influenced by Egypt. This intriguing nugget sheds light on what might have happened on Mount Sinai, when God wrote the Ten Commandments with His own finger on two tablets of stone, front and back, small enough for Moses to carry; after which, the prophet/lawgiver/friend of God got busy writing the Torah in the Hebrew language, using a phonetic alphabet. Forty years in the wilderness was a good opportunity to get this done.

Jesus referred to the Hebrew alphabet and the writing of Moses when he stated that not one "jot or tittle" (KJV) would disappear from the law until it was all fulfilled. This expression is similar to current jargon "dot your *i*'s and cross your *t*'s." Even the pen strokes used in Hebrew calligraphy are considered holy. In modern times, the handwritten scroll is still the most cherished format for the Hebrew Scriptures, the Original Testament.

The Hebrews avoided the custom of other ancient peoples whose rulers routinely destroyed accounts of their own defeats or that depicted their rivals in a favorable light. Some Egyptian artifacts from the biblical era actually show evidence of scratching out and reinscribing new information. The Original Testament, however, makes no attempt to avoid or cover over the Hebrews' defeats or humiliations; if anything, it emphasizes them. In fact, no ancient historical records exist that are more authentic than those in the Bible.

This authenticity is also demonstrated by the genealogies that are a regular feature of the biblical narrative, both OT and NT. Matthew begins his gospel with the geneology of the Messiah, which confirms that God kept the promise He gave to David, that the Messiah would be his descendent.

Until the discovery of the Dead Sea Scrolls in 1946, the earliest extant manuscript copy (book format rather than scroll) of the Hebrew Bible dated from the ninth century C̶E̶ AD). The Dead Sea Scrolls, written shortly before the birth in the stable, include copies of every book in the Bible except *Esther*. The ancient texts are word-for-word the same as the ninth-century manuscript, even though they are at least one thousand—that's one thousand—years older. (Check out Ketef Hinnom amulets for another very cool example of the Bible's antiquity.)

Every book in the Hebrew Bible is prophetic: about the Messiah, the nation of Israel, the Christian church, and/or world history. Many specific prophecies have already been fulfilled, and some are being fulfilled as we sit here. Examples include the reestablishment of the nation of Israel in one day, two thousand years after it was wiped off the map by the Romans. (The discovery of the Dead Sea Scrolls happened the same year.) The book of Isaiah describes in detail the Jews' return to their homeland 2,700 years before it happened. Other prophetic confirmations include the miraculous blooming of the Negev desert; transformation of wilderness into fertile farmland; and, even more remarkable, the rebirth of Hebrew as a first language, after having been dead for two thousand years, not spoken even by the Jews. Jesus told His disciples that their generation would witness the destruction of the temple, that not one stone would remain on another. This prophecy was fulfilled about forty years later when Rome eradicated the nation and demolished the temple in about AD 70, initiating the diaspora. This scattering of the Jews across the globe, an event unique in history, had also been prophesied.

Note:
In AD 79, about ten years after Rome's destruction of Jerusalem and the Second Temple, Mount Vesuvius erupted and buried the Roman resort city of Pompeii, preserving it for all time.

Another interesting tidbit: in Luke 12, Jesus tells his disciples,

> *There is nothing concealed that will not be disclosed, or hidden that will not be made known. What you have said in the dark will be heard in the daylight, and what you have whispered in the ear in the inner rooms will be proclaimed from the roofs.* (Luke 12:2–3)

Internet technology fulfills this prophecy in ways that were unimaginable at the time it was given, what the ancients would certainly consider a sign or wonder in the sky.

The term *New Testament* (or covenant) was first spoken by Jeremiah:

> *"The days are coming," declares the Lord, "when I will make a new testament with the people of Israel and with the people of Judah."* (Jer. 31:31)

Jesus announced the fulfillment of this prophecy at the Last Supper:

> *In the same way, after the supper he took the cup, saying, "This cup is the new covenant in my blood, which is poured out for you."* (Luke 22:20)

The whole canon of the New Testament was accepted and widely circulated within a few decades of the birth in the stable. First-century writers such as Polycarp—who was a student of John, the only apostle who had escaped martyrdom—Origen, Irenaeus, and other first-century writers discussed the four Gospels and the other texts so thoroughly in their writings that their quotes can be used to recreate the entire New Testament, except for fifteen verses at the end of *Mark*.

On the other hand, the so-called hidden gospels, such as the one known as The Gospel of Thomas, did not come to light until more than a century later and show clear evidence of several writers.

However, in spite of its unparalleled authenticity, belief in the truth of the Bible has all but disappeared from the American denominational church. Cultural trends and current events suggest this could be the result of its unvarnished depiction of God's violent retribution for disobedience, in addition to the Bible's definition, and condemnation, of sexual sin. Religious scholars continue to devise ingenious strategies to bypass these inconvenient passages, which are dismissed as mistranslated, outdated, obsolete, archaic, and/or irrelevant to twenty-first-century life.

The Bible, both the Original and the New Testament, is either all or nothing. Not accepting it in its entirety removes the foundation for leaning on any part of it. If the Pharaoh's plagues are unacceptable, so are the Beatitudes. If you can't stomach the idea of God's vengeance, then the reality of a redeeming savior is also lost.

Note:

The Exodus didn't happen in a vacuum. Contemporaneous sources reveal that ancient peoples nearby believed Pharaoh had expelled the Hebrews from Egypt because they carried plague. That explanation is reasonable and enhanced the fear of the Jews that spread over the area.

Agreement with certain portions of the Holy Scriptures, yoked to rejection of others, indicates no faith in any of it. Trusting human intellect to be the arbiter of truth is foolish; the whole horrific history of humanity is replete with the consequences of that ideology. *Homo sapiens* should have figured out by now that the most sophisticated intelligence cannot save us from ourselves or heal the planet that the Creator placed in our care.

The Creator is well able to safeguard the integrity of His Word. No nation has been more conscientious with its historical documents than the Jews, in spite of the fact that they had no homeland and were scattered all over the globe for more than twenty centuries. New evidence of the Bible's validity continues to appear with ongoing archaeological and literary revelations. The recent appearance of the Aramaic-English New Testament is one example.

The Bible is true on every level you can imagine: literal, figurative, symbolic, allegorical, scientific, archetypal, historical, political. This may be difficult to accept, surely, but the Creator is not limited to human understanding, and He transcends human intelligence. The Bible does not make God real; God, in His Word, supplies the code that makes the Bible real. Belief is a matter of choice. As a matter of fact, His mercy is so great even just wanting to believe can be enough, as manifested by the distraught father who brought his epileptic son to Jesus:

> *"Lord, I believe; help thou my unbelief!"* (Mark 9:24)

One may even assert that unbelief is the unforgivable sin.

Making an effort to become aquainted with the Bible, which is God's Word, and keeping an open mind to the teaching of the Holy Spirit, prepares your heart to receive His revelation, in the same way soil is prepared for the planting of crops. He Himself will help you. His communication will be personal, and His instruction will be individualized, exactly fitted for you and you alone. You will begin to realize the purpose of your own life.

> *"You will seek me and find me when you seek me with all your heart. I will be found by you," declares the Lord.* (Jer. 29:13–14)

> *"No longer will they teach their neighbor or say to one another, 'Know the Lord,' because they will all know me from the least of them to the greatest," declares the Lord.* (Jer. 31:34, quoted in Hebrews 8)

> *Ask and it will be given to you; seek and you will find; knock and the door will be opened to you. For everyone who asks receives; the one who seeks finds; and to the one who knocks, the door will be opened.* (Matt. 7:7–8)

Here's an assignment for you. The internet makes it easy.

1. Find translations of one or more of these scriptures of various religions:

    - *Quran* by Muhammad (Islam)
    - *Bhagavad Gita* by Vyasa (Hindu)
    - *Basic Writings* by Chuang Tzu (Taoism)
    - *Science and Health* by Mary Baker Eddy (Christian Science)
    - *Studies in the Scriptures* by Charles Taze Russell (Jehovah's Witnesses)
    - *The Book of Mormon* by Joseph Smith (Mormonism, Latter-day Saints)
    - *Dianetics* by L. Ron Hubbard (Scientology)

2. Choose one or more of these texts and read some: a chapter, a couple of pages, a section, enough to get a sense of its tone and meaning. If you're interested, read as much as you want.
3. Choose a book in the Bible and do a similar reading, following the same instructions.

- Keep an open, honest mind. (Don't lie to yourself.)
- Maintain intellectual integrity. (Don't accept useful lies to support your position.)
- Ask yourself: which one is real? (The use of fake King James English is a sure giveaway.)

Keeping your learning experiences between yourself and your heavenly Father, not discussing it unless He provides a specific opportunity, is a good skill to cultivate. If you have concerns, express them to Him. He already knows them all anyway. His responses will surprise and delight you, even though you would have a hard time trying to explain them to someone else.

Your Creator will continue to reveal Himself to you as long as you continue to believe Him and put into practice what He reveals to you. Why would He communicate with someone who thinks he can disobey if he disagrees with the message?

First of all: set your will to obey Him. Don't worry, He knows how to make Himself perfectly clear; He, and only He, understands the secret language of your heart, which you have up to now been using to deceive yourself. (More about this elsewhere.) He will meet you there, in your secret place. Be prepared, because **truth is the only language you can speak with God.** Also, be forewarned: obedience to God requires courage and personal sacrifice, a significant portion of which will be totally unknown to everyone but Him. But **God never rejects anybody.** Anybody who cries, "Lord, help!" gets help.

The one thing you can't do is try it out just to see if it works.

CHAPTER 3

Forsaken God

In the beginning, God created the heavens and the earth.

—Gen. 1:1

You shall have no other gods before me.

—Deut. 5:7

Love the Lord your God with all your heart and with all your soul and with all your strength.

—Deut. 6:5

The Bible asserts in several places that the fear of the Lord is the beginning of wisdom (Job 28:28; Ps. 111:10; Prov. 1:7). It is also identified as humility (Prov. 22:4) and the key to hidden treasure (Isa. 33:6).

Paradoxically—as so much of God's Word is, kind of like the way quantum theory relates to Newtonian physics—fearing the "God of the Old Testament" might be the first indication that truth picked up my Bible, opening it on the chapter for the day—Luke chapter 11—and this is what greeted my eyes:

> *One day Jesus was praying in a certain place.* [what I was just doing] *When he finished, one of his disciples said to him, "Lord, teach us to pray,* [the need that I had just expressed] *just as John taught his disciples." He said to them, "When you pray, say: 'Father, hallowed be your name.'"*

That's as far as I got. I have known the Lord's Prayer by heart since I was a preschooler, but I was seeing this for the first time. The first thing we should pray, in any situation, is that His Name would be revered. It's also the third commandment. (Christians, unlike believers in any other faith, are <u>instructed</u> to call God "Father.")

* * * * *

How many times a day do you guess God's name is blasphemed here in the USA?

Using expressions like "Jesus Christ" and "God damn it" as expletives expressing shock, pain, or frustration might not be among the most serious abuses of His Name, considering that it is routinely exploited as a means of gaining people's trust in order to take their money or get their votes. His name is regularly used to manipulate people, not because the speaker believes in Him but because the speaker thinks the audience does. A spouse can use the name of the Lord as a psychological billy club to maintain superiority in the home. His name is used as a gimmick to sell religious materials in the church's Bible bookstore, marketed as a means of helping you to draw closer to Him.

Churchgoers would do well to remember how Jesus reacted to the businessmen at the temple, who were selling worshippers the items necessary for participation in the temple services (see Matthew chapter 21). God <u>always</u> blesses innocent believers who are sincerely seeking Him through whatever means they can find, but "Bible teachers"—who God holds to a higher standard—offering slickly produced workbooks and study guides for sale, charging significant speaking fees, and/or using media (social and otherwise) to encourage contributions to their cause, had better open their eyes before it is too late. And it is getting very late.

Note:

One popular teacher some years back called her method "Precept upon Precept," somehow missing the fact that in Isaiah 28, where this phrase originates, it is identified as a shameful, not praiseworthy, state of affairs. Because someone offers a beautifully published daily devotional guide doesn't mean he knows what he is talking about. Again, **no one should be dependent on someone else's Bible reading.**

* * * * *

Some misuse His name by claiming that He has spoken to them in order to gain the admiration of other churchgoers, who are a valuable peer group. Some ignorant souls have "gone into ministry" because they think being a pastor would be a secure and not very taxing career path. Churchgoers, to whom dishonesty and deceit are customary practices during the week, recite the Apostle's Creed, the Priestly Benediction, the Lord's Prayer, "in Thy name we pray" or even "in Jesus's name we pray," as a kind of incantation, without fear of God and not a shred of reverence for His name. They are practicing superstition, not faith. Of course, once the "God of the Old Testament" has been canceled, there's no more reason to fear that bogeyman, right?

Consider this:

Using the phrase "in the name of Jesus" to validate a "prayer" that is actually a sermonette, is blasphemy. The others may not recognize it, but you can be sure God does. In fact, it's quite possible that you yourself are guilty but don't realize it. Until now.

Frankly, Sunday morning is probably when God's name is abused most.

* * * * *

Simply examining the use of the word *God*, and the concepts it represents, can lead into a dense web of connotations, denotations, translations, and interpretations. The Bible, God's written Word, is, as always, the ultimate standard to confirm or refute other sources.

The first word translated "god" in the Bible, *Elohim,* appears in the first verse of the first book, Genesis 1:1 and undeniably refers to the Creator of the universe. It's a unique pluralization of the Semitic *el,* a term commonly used to mean "god" among the Abrahamic tribes occupying the Middle East at the time *Genesis* was being written. *El* would normally be expressed in the singular; the pluralization *Elohim* is suggestive of "God of all gods."

Note:

Abraham, Isaac, and Jacob (renamed Israel by God) are the patriarchs of the Hebrew nation. However, Abrahamic tribes also include descendants of Abraham's half Egyptian son Ishmael, as well as descendents of Jacob's twin brother, Esau, who intermarried with Ishmael's descendants. The lines of Ishmael and Esau, both migrating into the East (one of those significant details), commingled, and became the progenitors of the Arab peoples—those "begats" can be more interesting than you might at first suppose—thus, the bitter Arab-Israeli sibling rivalry has continued since the dawn of history. Keep in mind, though, that the Arabs share knowledge that was transmitted from Abraham, notably about the one God, the prophesied Messiah, and the Mazzaroth, which in Greek is termed zodiac. (More about this elsewhere.)

The opening verses of *Genesis* might be problematic for a well-educated skeptic, but real scientific discoveries (not theories) often disclose biblical truth. In fact, our Creator has engineered every detail of the material universe to reveal Himself to us.

In the beginning [time], *Elohim* [God of all gods] *created* [made from nothing] *the heavens* [space] *and the earth* [matter]. (Gen. 1:1)

The God of the Hebrew Bible, which is also known as the ~~Old~~ Original Testament, is the CREATOR.

Now the earth was formless and empty [an incomprehensible but finite number of lifeless disorganized particles], *darkness was over the surface of the deep and the Spirit of God* [energy] *was hovering* [vibrating] *over the waters.* (Gen.1:2)

Genesis is always included in the literary canon of "creation stories," but none of the other accounts even pretend to approach reality. No other account begins with nothing and addresses the sophisticated concepts of time, space, matter, and energy. Although the serpent speaks in the Bible story, he is clearly very different from the talking animals who appear in almost all mythology from around the globe, including Native American. *Genesis* also avoids the use of fantastic elements, such as Hindu's three lotus petals growing from the creative energy of Lord Vishnu's navel.

Creation and flood stories from around the world share common elements, but many linguistic historians maintain that the *Genesis* account is the original, from which the others diverge and derive. In other words, the Hindu and the Taoist (for example) versions allude to older details from *Genesis*, not vice versa. Interestingly, in many creation myths, the serpent, or dragon, appears as the predominant "good" force. This is not surprising when judged from the perspective of the biblical account, which depicts the serpent as a deceiver seeking to supplant the authority of the Creator.

The use of the first-person plural *Elohim* is also an expression of the triune character of the Godhead: Creator, Spirit, Word, in addition to "God of all gods," mentioned earlier. This is an example of how a Bible passage can express more than one truth at a time.

> *And God said, "Let there be light," and there was light.* (Gen. 1:3)

God spoke—He projected a very particular type of sound energy into the chaos of particles: the vibrations were configured in such a way as to communicate meaning, which is what we call speech. When God speaks, new things, things that were not, come into being. In this instance, photons appear in the morass of particles, immediately instigating an explosion of activity, and hey, presto! The big bang.

More than twenty other Bible verses identify the presence of God with light.

> *God is light, and in Him there is no darkness at all.* (1 John 1:5)
>
> (a biblical defined metaphor; more about that in Part 10)

God reveals something of His nature and His plan in everything He creates.

> *For since the creation of the world God's invisible qualities—his eternal power and divine nature—have been clearly seen, being understood from what has been made, so that people are without excuse.* (Rom. 1:20)

Scoffers dismiss the Bible for its "contradictions," but *paradoxes* is the appropriate term. A good example is the familiar long-standing debate about Christian salvation: is it free will, or predestination?

A correlation can be found in the nature of light: is it a particle (predestination), or a wave (free will)? Well, it depends. Who is observing? What standard of measurement is being used? What instruments are used to make the measurement? When and how is it being observed? (reminiscent of the old *Saturday Night Live* skit: "Is it a floor wax or a dessert topping? You're both right!"). The fact that a paradox exists, that some details appear contradictory, or can't be explained, doesn't negate the validity of the phenomenon. And, at one and the same time, the speed of those contrary light particles in a vacuum is also a universal constant, which can be utilized to understand and master our environment, even beyond our own planet.

The force that causes objects to hang together in space is gravity, the other constant. Gravity is consistent and easily calculated. Because of gravity, electrons cling to protons, atoms form molecules, planets orbit stars, moons orbit planets, and galaxies continue their graceful ballet across space. Because of gravity's reliability, humans can not only design rockets that launch satellites into space with almost pinpoint accuracy but also, closer to home, manufacture airplanes that provide dependable transportation. Gravity keeps all the particles in the universe behaving exactly as they should to maintain a habitat in which humans thrive, but no scientist on earth can explain why. Consider these verses:

> *He upholds all things by the word of His power.* (Heb. 1:3)

> *He is before all things, and in Him all things hold together.* (Col. 1:17)

He holds the worlds together by the Word of His power. Gravity is the Word of His power.

> *For this is what the LORD says—He who created the heavens; He is God; He who fashioned and made the earth, He founded it; He did not create it to be empty, but formed it to be inhabited—He says, "I am the LORD, and there is no other."* (Isa. 45:18)

All this is, as He said Himself, good; but He is even more than the Creator of the universe.

No scientist has yet brought an inanimate molecule to life. Even so, many confidently assert that life was the result of a lucky electrical shock under just the right conditions. Then, once that ball was rolling, only time was needed to eventually produce mankind and his wonderful environment. The time necessary was at first postulated as possibly millions, then billions, and now trillions of years. Nature and science documentaries report this time line as if it were established fact; it's the only way that the evolutionary model has even a ghost of a chance for reality. But the alternative is so frightening schoolchildren are being protected from even finding out what it is.

To be honest, believing that life resulted from a lightning strike into a primordial soup of mixed particles takes a great deal of faith, and even more faith—blind, deaf, and dumb faith—to believe that eventually, the resulting life form would begin reproducing itself.

God is the Creator, who brings something out of nothing. He is the God who made the heavens. In Him we live, move, and have our being. He made everything that is. He established physical laws to maintain order in the cosmos, and spiritual laws to govern eternity: the reality that each person knows, in our own deepest self, our own heart of hearts, to exist, even though it is not detected by any of our five senses.

The Creator, your Creator, is the only one who understands the secret language of your heart. In fact, He knows it better than you do.

Why do we call Him Father instead of Mother? Because Jesus told us to. As a matter of fact, Christianity is the only faith system that instructs believers to call God "Father." That's what got the Messiah executed. Those concerned about misogyny in the Bible need look no further than Genesis chapter 3 to discover that the Messiah Himself would come from the seed of the woman; later on in the New Testament, the church (men, women, everybody) is designated the bride of Christ. A number of references to the Creator as a female entity (a hen gathering her chicks, a nursing mother, and the like) are found throughout the Bible, but would not be obvious to someone just skimming along looking for proof texts.

The *Genesis* creation account addresses not only the phenomenon of life itself but, even more astounding, living beings sorted into "kinds" that can reproduce. (So, obviously, the chicken came first.)

He is the Creator. He is light. He is the author of <u>life that reproduces itself</u>.

Throughout the book of *Genesis*, individuals who encounter God tend to give Him a name based on what He has done for them, using *El* along with some other descriptive term, such as *the God who sees* or *the God who provides*. Isn't this just like us? Never mind being the Creator; You see me, You provide for me, and that's what's important. Me.

And then...we come to the book of *Exodus*, when Moses does something unprecedented. During the episode at the burning bush, Moses courageously asks God what He should be called, and God responds: I AM WHO I AM, which is actually more accurately translated:

> *I WILL BE WHO I WILL BE*
> *This is my name forever,*
> *the name you shall call me*
> *from generation to generation.*

<u>God tells us to use His name</u>. Take a moment to look through the book of Psalms and note the many references to God's name, for example, *"The Name of the Lord is a strong tower / the righteous run into and are safe."*

You might already know that the Hebrew alphabet contains only consonants, and that God's name is spelled, using the English alphabet, YHWH, known as the tetragrammaton. The pronunciation, with vowels included, is often spelled Y-A-H-W-E-H. Try this: keep your mouth slightly open and slowly pronounce the name Yahweh, "Yah" exhaling, "weh" inhaling. You are pronouncing His name each time you draw breath, first exhaling, then inhaling. Communion with God begins with expelling the negative, whatever is sin (dishonesty); after that, refilling with the positive, the true, His divine nature. Out with the bad air, in with the good. Confess and be healed.

If we confess our sins, he is faithful and just and will forgive us our sins and purify us from all unrighteousness. (1 John 1:9)

The human term *God* turns out to be a woefully inadequate title for the Creator.

God's existence is not dependent on or defined by interaction with humans. And yet, in American churches, the overriding priority is making God and the Bible "relevant" to people's daily lives because few will show up unless they get some kind of tangible personal benefit from it. (A couple of hours of free, guiltless childcare counts.) The God of the ~~Old~~ Original Testament is not a popular topic; in fact, "I just can't believe in the God of the Old Testament" is a statement often heard in conversations about God, even—or especially—among churchgoers, otherwise labeled "good Christians" in the community. And if they don't show up at the erroneously labeled "worship" service, they're not likely to give up any of their money, and the building fund will suffer a serious setback. BUT He's the Creator. He is light. He is the author of reproductive life.

You have no input into what God is like. None.
He is who He is.
He will be who He will be.

The Creator of the universe doesn't need human affirmation or validation. Quite the reverse. God, who creates each person in His own image, is also each person's judge. Jesus told his listeners to fear Him who can cast your soul into hell (Luke 12:5, Matt. 10:28). God's judgments are true; He is justified in His wrath toward mankind, which includes you and me. The correlating spiritual law can be stated like Newton's Third Law of Motion and Aristotle's similar expression:

- Every action (sin, evil) is met by an equal and opposite reaction (God's vengeance, wrath, judgment).
- Nature abhors a vacuum.

In both of these events, there can't <u>not</u> be a reaction. Empty space cannot be sustained; when compromised, the space fills immediately until it balances the surrounding environment. The space, when compromised, can't <u>not</u> be filled.

Sin provokes God's wrath, and His wrath cannot be restrained.

Our privileged nation is populated by millions who do not respect God and are not grateful for His provision but, instead, totally motivated by self-interest, participate in all kinds of evil. His warnings are clear. He is not sneaking up on anybody.

The Bible states more than once that God mocks and laughs at, and is even sarcastic toward, His enemies.

> *Why do the nations conspire and the peoples plot in vain? The kings of the earth rise up and the rulers band together against the Lord and against his anointed, saying, "Let us break their chains and throw off their shackles."*
>
> *The One enthroned in heaven laughs; the Lord scoffs at them. He rebukes them in his anger and terrifies them in his wrath, saying, "I have installed my king on Zion, my holy mountain."*
>
> *I will proclaim the Lord's decree: He said to me, "You are my son; today I have become your father. Ask me, and I will make the nations your inheritance, the ends of the earth your possession. You will break them with a rod of iron; you will dash them to pieces like pottery."*
>
> *Therefore, you kings, be wise; be warned, you rulers of the earth. Serve the Lord with fear and celebrate his rule with trembling. Kiss his son, or he will be angry and your way will lead to your destruction, for his wrath can flare up in a moment. Blessed are all who take refuge in him.* (Ps. 2)

> *I form the light and create darkness, I bring prosperity and create disaster; I, the Lord, do all these things.*
>
> *"You heavens above, rain down my righteousness; let the clouds shower it down. Let the earth open wide, let salvation spring up, let righteousness flourish with it; I, the Lord, have created it.*
>
> *"Woe to those who quarrel with their Maker, those who are nothing but potsherds among the potsherds on the ground. Does the clay say to the potter, 'What are you making?' Does your work say, 'The potter has no hands?'* (Isa. 45:7–9)

Nietzsche famously asserted: "God is dead. God remains dead. And we have killed him." Everyone is careful to point out that what the philosopher meant was that God's influence had been erased from public life. Here's the thing: If it was killed, or erased, it wasn't the Creator to begin with.

> *But God made the earth by his power He founded the world by his wisdom and stretched out the heavens by his understanding. When he thunders, the waters in the heavens roar; he makes clouds rise from the ends of the earth. He sends lightning with the rain and brings out the wind from his storehouses.* (Jer. 10:12–13)
>
> *The heavens declare the glory of God; the skies proclaim the work of his hands. Day after day they pour forth speech; night after night they display knowledge.* (Ps. 19:1–2)

God reveals Himself through His creation, which never stops broadcasting His love. Every detail in nature teaches something about Him; He is the Creator of life that reproduces its own kind.

This truth is emphasized throughout the Bible, Original and New Testaments, as the foundation of the gospel.

> *We are bringing you good news, telling you to turn from these worthless things to the living God, who made the heavens and the earth and the sea and everything in them.* (Acts 14:15)

> *For since the creation of the world God's invisible qualities—his eternal power and divine nature—have been clearly seen, being understood from what has been made, so that people are without excuse.* (Rom. 1:20)

There is but one God, the Father, from whom all things came and for whom we live; and there is but one Lord, Jesus Christ, through whom all things came and through whom we live. (1 Cor. 8:6)

> *For every house is built by someone, but God is the builder of everything.* (Heb. 3:4)

> *And he swore by Him who lives for ever and ever, who created the heavens and all that is in them, the earth and all that is in it, and the sea and all that is in it.* (Rev. 10:6)

Anyone who fails to acknowledge the God of the Original Testament can make no claim to the Christian faith. Without the Creator and His justified vengeance, there is no need for Christ and no Christianity. Nothing is more foolish than to forget—or ignore—who God is.

> *The fool has said in his heart, "There is no God."* (Ps. 53:1)

More assignments, same instructions as before:

Google "global creation stories." Read as many as you like. Then, read Genesis chapters 1–3. Which is real?

Do the same with "global flood stories." (Noah appears in the Hebrew Bible in Genesis chapters 5–9.)

Remember:

Honest, open mind.

Intellectual integrity.

CHAPTER 4

Forsaken Man

Then God said, "Let us make mankind in our image, in our likeness, so that they may rule over the fish in the sea and the birds in the sky, over the livestock and all the wild animals, and over all the creatures that move along the ground."
—Gen. 1:26

Jesus reminded his disciples of the power that God originally intended man to wield as His steward over creation: *"Truly I tell you, if you have faith as small as a mustard seed, you can say to this mountain, 'Move from here to there,' and it will move. Nothing will be impossible for you"* (Matt. 17:20). This verse is often translated in a way that implies faith the same size as a mustard seed, but a more accurate rendering might be the same amount of faith that a mustard seed has. Power resides in agreement with God; He intends that nothing be impossible for His children.

The conscious decision to surrender to God, in that instant being absolutely honest (therefore deeply ashamed) and saying yes to your Maker, recognizing who He is and who you are, initiates the new birth and opens the door to eternal life. In the Sermon on the Mount, Jesus told the listeners,

> *"You are the light of the world."* (Matt. 5:14)

Paul also emphasizes this precept in his letters; two notable examples are the following:

> *For you were once darkness, but now you are light in the Lord. Live as children of light.* (Eph. 5:8)

> *You are all children of the light and children of the day. We do not belong to the night or to the darkness.* (1 Thess. 5:5)

Set aside your disbelief and consider the words. What could this mean? What do the words say, without adding or subtracting or interpreting? What does it mean for humanity that our species alone receives life from the breath of God, who is light? What does it mean that we were created in His image, He who is light? Why? This is seriously not like a myth.

The phrase "and God said" is repeated seven times in the first chapter of Genesis. From the beginning, language expresses God's creative force; He speaks, and it happens. When the sound energy in God's voice acted on the material universe, worlds came into being. Mankind is created in His image, and this astonishing power has been conferred on us as well.

The Creator entrusted man with the significant responsibility for naming every other living thing—even the woman—using spoken language to identify and define anything "not man." Adam functioned as someone distinct from, and superior to, all other created beings. Spoken language is unique to the human species and is made possible through the use of highly specified multifunctioning organs: sinuses, cheeks, mouth, lips, teeth, tongue, lungs, and diaphragm, as well as cognitive ability not found in any other creature. Man was made to talk.

Human words are creative, just as God's are. When humans speak words, things happen whether we want them to or not. Every time a word leaves a mouth, the surrounding atmosphere is affected for good or ill, and that effect can never be undone. God has given us dominion, and even the weakest of us can control our personal space. Nothing is more powerful than the right word in the right place; a truthful and sincere apology is quite possibly the most forceful game changer at our disposal. On the other hand, a phony apology can be used as an easy—perhaps even cowardly—way to maintain peace, which is then also phony.

However, the wrong word is also powerful, and once released, it can never be unsaid. A person's use of words can inspire emotions that compel action, say, a riot; or, on the other end of the spectrum, human language can transmit forgiveness or bring peace and comfort where there was none before. On the other hand, language can also be manipulated to benefit the unscrupulous and victimize the innocent. This creative ability is bestowed on no other living species; it is man's, alone. Each of us needs to take this seriously; words are powerful, even the unpremeditated ones.

Robert Sapolsky, a popular neuroscientist and TED Talk contributor, identifies himself as a "strident atheist," yet even he concedes that mankind is not like other creatures. In his talk, "The Uniqueness of Humans," he notes that there are serious problems with including humans in the animal world as a species. He points out that human beings are unremarkable in their physical abilities, but have found ways to use those abilities that are unmatched by any other being. Sapolsky states that humans "have no precedent in the animal world." (Does the biblical record account for this? Why, yes, it does.)

The most astounding human characteristic, according to Sapolsky, is that we are capable of "magnificent irrationality." He notes that this is a particularly apt description of the Christian moral imperative to love the unlovable, forgive the unforgivable, and wait until after death to be rewarded. The behavior of those who live according to this moral imperative is illogical. (He can be excused for misunderstanding the Christian concept of death and the timing of Christian rewards.)

Humans also have other peculiar characteristics. For one thing, we love beauty; it's not necessary for survival, but people have been collecting beautiful items from earliest times. We have an innate desire for beauty and will sacrifice other more necessary pursuits, sometimes even to the point of self-endangerment, to pursue it. Prehistoric necessities such as clothing, tools, and shelter, became the maker's opportunity to invent pleasing decoration. Humans also create works of art for no other reason than to create art; we wear jewelry for no good reason.

We also dance at every opportunity and again for no good reason. Even infants respond to rhythm by moving their limbs and toddlers bounce up and down, so of course, we learned to compose music and invent instruments to play it. Humans are also aware of a supernatural reality outside our material existence. One scholar suggested that instead of *Homo sapiens*, we should be called *Homo religioso*. We have an inherent predisposition to worship.

In the biblical creation account, human beings are not included in any other animal groups that are mentioned: sea creatures, birds, wild animals, domesticated animals, or creeping things. According to Genesis, God created human beings to inhabit the earth and to rule over the rest of creation.

> *God blessed them and said to them, "Be fruitful and increase in number; fill the earth and subdue it. Rule over the fish in the sea and the birds in the sky and over every living creature that moves on the ground."* (Gen. 1:28)

God made the earth to be man's habitat. Man wasn't designed to be idle; he would have productive work to do and a beautiful landscape in which to do it. God gave man dominion over the rest of creation; humans cannot be like the other species, but like God. No other creation story makes anywhere near such an audacious claim.

Man is a biological animal, certainly, but he is also something far more, completely different from other animals.

> *To Adam he said, "Because you listened to your wife and ate fruit from the tree about which I commanded you, 'You must not eat from it,'" "Cursed is the ground because of you; through painful toil you will eat food from it all the days of your life. It will produce thorns and thistles for you, and you will eat the plants of the field. By the sweat of your brow you will eat your food until you return to the ground, since from it you were taken; for dust you are and to dust you will return."* (Gen. 3:17–19)

The earth is still suffering the consequences of Adam's abdication of his authority. Sufficient food can no longer be obtained by the pleasant tending of the garden; now, providing food is possible only through physical labor. The curse of physical death ensured that the living cells of the human body, and all other living things, became subject to decay and death, doomed to decompose into the elements that had been used to make them.

Many people find this position of authority so intimidating that they weave complex mental shrouds to cover over their inherent responsibility. They convince themselves that human beings are, really, not all that superior to other creatures. They reason that animals have abilities we don't and are not capable of evil as we are. A new cultural buzzword is *sentient*, meaning self-aware, a quality ascribed to various animals that makes them, if not exactly equal to humans, at least unacceptable for the dinner table. A recent species nominated for this distinction is the octopus, possibly due to a wonderful documentary created by a marine biologist who developed a close relationship with a female octopus that lasted until she (the octopus) died.

Animal rights activists are not an unfamiliar or unwelcome presence in the United States. Wildlife experts such as Jane Goodall enjoy a respected status in our culture; Francine Patterson made Koko the gorilla a household name, claiming that Koko had learned to understand two thousand spoken words, as well as more than one thousand terms in "Gorilla Sign Language." Many other cases of human interactions with animals demonstrate that animals can thrive and exhibit unnaturally (supernaturally?) advanced behaviors when knowledgeable humans care for them. People seem to coalesce into two undesirable groups when it comes to interacting with our natural habitat: a quest for material wealth with no regard for the consequences; or a compulsion to pacify a guilty conscience, believing that all authority is oppression.

> *Do not be afraid of those who kill the body but cannot kill the soul. Rather, be afraid of the One who can destroy both soul and body in hell. Are not two sparrows sold for a penny? Yet not one of them will fall to the ground outside your Father's care. And even the very hairs of your head are all numbered. So don't be afraid; you are worth more than many sparrows.* (Matt. 10:28–31)

Dominion is not the same thing as oppression; dominion is stewardship based on love. The Bible says that all creation groans in expectation of the manifestion of the sons of God. God-given dominion is good, and right, and necessary for a healthy environment.

CHAPTER 5
Forsaken Family

Gen. 5:2 Male and female, created he them.
—Gen. 5:2

Then God said, "Let us make man in our image, in our likeness, so that they may rule over the fish in the sea and the birds in the sky, over the livestock and all the wild animals, and over all the creatures that move along the ground."
So God created man in his own image,
In the image of God he created them
Male and female he created them.
God blessed them and said to them, "<u>Be fruitful and increase in number; fill the earth and subdue it.</u> Rule over the fish in the sea and the birds in the sky and over every living creature that moves on the ground."
—Gen. 1:26–28

God created man because He wanted to be a father. Like every good father would want to do, He provided His children with a comfortable home that met their needs. His intention from the beginning was to have planet Earth serve as the habitat for the proliferation of human families, all created in His image, eternally expanding in all directions like a fractal.

> *Then the Lord God formed a man from the dust of the ground and breathed into his nostrils the breath of life, and the man became a living being.* (Gen. 2:7)
>
> *The Lord God said, "It is not good for the man to be alone. I will make a helper suitable for him." Now the Lord God had formed out of the ground all the wild animals and all the birds in the sky. He brought them to the man to see what he would name them; and whatever the man called each living creature, that was its name. So the man gave names to all the livestock, the birds in the sky and all the wild animals. But for Adam no suitable helper was found. So the Lord God caused the man to fall into a deep sleep; and while he was sleeping, he took one of the man's ribs and then closed up the place with flesh. Then the Lord God made a woman from the rib he had taken out of the man, and he brought her to the man. The man said, "This is now bone of my bones and flesh of my flesh; she shall be called 'woman,' for she was taken out of man." That is why a man leaves his father and motherand is united to his wife, and they become one flesh. Adam and his wife were both naked, and they felt no shame.* (Gen. 2:18–25)

God deemed every work of creation good, until the creation of man. He had created man to have a family of His own kind, to love as a part of Himself. Then, He pronounced that it was not good for man to be alone; Adam needed someone to love, just as His Creator did. God continued the pattern and provided a woman for him, bone of his bone and flesh of his flesh.

<u>God's first institution on earth was human marriage.</u>

The scripture above is the first reference to marriage in the Bible. Jesus quoted this verse a couple of thousand years later in his answer to a Pharisee's question about divorce. The union of husband and wife requires the separation of each from their original family unit in order to establish a new strand. In his letter to the Ephesians, Paul writes,

> *For this reason I kneel before the Father, from whom every family in heaven and on earth derives its name.* (Eph. 3:14–15)

The union of male and female is featured in the first chapter of the Bible and the last; the entire book known as *Song of Songs,* or *Song of Solomon,* is dedicated to its celebration; the book of *Proverbs* devotes three entire chapters, with other verses scattered throughout, with advice about sexual behavior and successful marriages, not forgetting *Proverbs* 31, the definitive acclamation of a good wife. The historical accounts of *Ruth* and *Esther* record the heroic behavior of women in entirely different circumstances whose behavior as wives saved the Hebrew people from annihilation and provided a link in the genealogy of the Messiah. Chapter 2 of *Malachi,* the final book of the Original Testament, the last prophetic message for four hundred years, does not mince words:

> *Another thing you do: You flood the Lord's altar with tears. You weep and wail because he no longer looks with favor on your offerings or accepts them with pleasure from your hands. You ask, "Why?" It is because the Lord is the witness between you and the wife of your youth. You have been unfaithful to her, though she is your partner, the wife of your marriage covenant. Has not the one God made you?*

> *You belong to him in body and spirit. And <u>what does the one God seek? Godly offspring</u>. So be on your guard, and do not be unfaithful to the wife of your youth. "The man who hates and divorces his wife," says the Lord, the God of Israel, "does violence to the one he should protect," says the Lord Almighty. So be on your guard, and do not be unfaithful.* (Mal. 2:13–16)

In the New Testament, Jesus's first miracle, turning water to wine, took place at a wedding. John the Baptist identified Jesus as the bridegroom (a biblical defined metaphor). Jesus identified Himself as the bridegroom. The final scene in the Bible is the wedding of the lamb to His bride, the church, the New Jerusalem. This is as significant as it gets.

The Bible's preeminent metaphor, anchoring the entire saga of God's relationship with humankind, is the relationship between male and female, whose union is the origin of family.

God intends human marriage to be the earthly demonstration of His eternal character, His reclamation of believers into His own family, partaking of His divine nature.

Forget about the influence of sin for now. Everything about marital love is meant to disclose something about God's love. In the Bible, the male/husband/bridegroom signifies God/Christ, and the female/wife/bride signifies the church/body of Christ. Even, or perhaps especially, human sexual intercourse reveals how God's love manifests itself. Humans, unlike other species, regularly participate in intercourse face-to-face. The male partner must be patient and sensitive to his wife's needs, controlling his own desire; the female partner must be willing to expose her most acute vulnerability and allow herself to be invaded. Both must deny their own most basic instincts. In the same way, God remains patient with us, continually expressing His love, until we are ready to step into His light and invite Him into the private place of our hearts, where He deposits His reproductive life.

Stepping into His light enables you to become a child of God, to discover your own purpose in life, being educated by the teaching, counsel, and comfort of the Holy Spirit. Saying yes to the Creator and being born of the Spirit equips each person with the ability to escape the bondage of self and to walk in His light. Only after being born by the Spirit is anyone capable of making decisions outside the influence of his own schema or his own sinful nature. Merely recognizing one's own biases requires supernatural help. (More about this elsewhere.) The sacrificial death of the Lord Jesus Christ, Yeshua HaMashiach, makes this possible. In other words, it is not possible to be objective about yourself until your sin has been covered by the blood of Jesus.

As male and female human beings, God has designed us specifically for the profound function of procreation: participating in the creation of unique living persons <u>who are made in God's image.</u> Research has consistently supported the heterosexual monogamous nuclear family as the best situation for a family in which children, the natural outcome of sexual love, thrive. (Remember, sin is out of the picture.) Its exclusive nature fosters a strong bond among the parents and their offspring. No research has ever indicated that there is a healthier option for human life, not only for children but also for adults. Because heterosexual monogamy—the conjoining of male and female—is such a spiritual powerhouse, it has been from the very beginning the predominant target of our adversary, the devil.

A primary desire of sinful man (quite likely <u>the</u> primary desire), enthusiastically promoted by the enemy, is to be able to have sex with anyone, anytime. All of Satan's wiles are based on falsehoods; lying really is the only arrow in his quiver. In this case, the big lie is that life without good sex is not worth living. A satisfying climax is the whole point of existence, the most wonderful experience life offers. Orgasms make the rest of life worthwhile. Every human pursuit becomes a means of acquiring satisfactory sexual experiences, from blue pills to hair dye to gym memberships, including the ascent of the corporate ladder. Medical interventions make it possible to continue having sex long after the physical body has decided to move on, because after all, if you're not anticipating the next climax, you might as well be dead. Right?

Sacrificing the security of defenseless children on the altar of good sex is commonplace in our society. Escaping a "loveless" marriage (dull, predictable intercourse?) is considered reasonable, even necessary, for the mental health of a parent, regardless of the consequences to the mental health of the children. Some assert that a marriage should not be expected to continue only for the sake of the children. On the contrary, the children's well-being is the <u>best</u> reason to stay married. The big lie is that "love"—manifested by mutual climaxes—is ephemeral and must be seized whenever possible. The truth is that love is a choice, manifested by behavior. Spouses choose to love each other, and they make conscious decisions every day to actively express that love, no matter what they feel.

* * * * *

Colorful graphic depictions of DNA strands are often included in textbooks and other commonly used resources, so their configuration is not unfamiliar. Here's an ancient but uncannily accurate metaphor:

> *For you created my inmost being; you knit me together in my mother's womb.* (Ps. 139:13)

When a man and a woman become one flesh (spouses of one another), a new family is established, and the whole is greater than the sum of the parts. The combined DNA forms the basis for an unprecedented strand of unique human beings made in the image of God.

> *The word of the Lord came to me, saying, 'Before I formed you in the womb I knew you, before you were born I set you apart'* (Jer. 1:4–5)

is making inroads into the house of cards known as your psyche (also called your secret place, inner man, heart, persona, schema, or spirit; more about this elsewhere). The third commandment specifically instructs us not to abuse or misuse His name. In fact, the Bible warns that no one who misuses His name will go unpunished. When God says people will not go unpunished, He means it.

Note:

The Bible contains 1,189 chapters of widely varying lengths, which can be covered in 1 1/2 years by reading two chapters a day. At the same pace, seven completions would take about a decade. Reading these chapters as part of a daily routine, like taking vitamins, is far more effective at internalizing the content than topic or word studies. God's Word works to strengthen the spirit as vitamins work to strengthen the body. (Regular exercise is more effective at improving fitness than studying about muscle tone.) Of course, it is also being absorbed by your conscious memory as well. And, furthermore, the Holy Spirit will bring it to your remembrance when you need it.

> "All this I have spoken while still with you. But the Advocate, the Holy Spirit, whom the Father will send in my name, will teach you all things and will remind you of everything I have said to you. Peace I leave with you; my peace I give you. I do not give to you as the world gives. Do not let your hearts be troubled and do not be afraid." (John 14:25–27)

A personal anecdote:

Many years ago, during a season of intense trial, I had gone out on the tiny balcony outside our bedroom, which was where I liked to pray. I considered the stars and thought, *Oh my God, look at what you have made. How can I presume to tell you what my problems are? You know everything already. I don't even know how to pray. All I ask right now is that You speak to me. I don't care what You say, just speak to me.* (That's pretty close to word-for-word.) I went into the bedroom and

> *And He has <u>made from one blood every nation of men</u> to dwell on all the face of the earth, and has determined their preappointed times and the boundaries of their dwellings, so that they should seek the Lord, in the hope that they might grope for Him and find Him, though He is not far from each one of us; for in Him we live and move and have our being, as also some of your own poets have said, "For we are also His offspring." (Acts 17:26–28)*

Race, never mentioned in the Bible, is an artificial classification established by men for their own purposes. The biblical use of the term *kind* indicates the ability to mate and produce fertile offspring. For example, horses and donkeys are not the same "kind," because even though they can mate, their offspring, the useful mule, cannot reproduce. Obviously, all human beings are one kind.

> *Adam named his wife Eve, because she would become the mother of all the living. (Gen. 3:20)*

Adam's naming of his wife is an expression of his authority—remember, authority does not mean oppression—over her. Jesus refers to this in Matthew 19:

> *Some Pharisees came to him to test him. They asked, 'Is it lawful for a man to divorce his wife for any and every reason?' "Haven't you read," he replied, "that at the beginning the Creator 'made them male and female,' and said, 'For this reason a man will leave his father and mother and be united to his wife, and the two will become one flesh'? So they are no longer two, but one flesh. Therefore what God has joined together, let no one separate." (Matt.19:3–6)*

<u>God specified only two categories of human: male and female.</u> The designation is entirely dependent on physical attributes at birth:

females have ovaries that produce eggs; males have testes that produce sperm. Sperm and egg are both necessary for the creation of a new life. Each human baby is a unique individual, created in the image of God, and conception can happen only one way: the union of male sperm and female egg. This could not be any simpler.

> *Has not the one God made you? You belong to him in body and spirit. And what does the one God seek? Godly offspring. So be on your guard, and do not be unfaithful to the wife of your youth.* (Mal. 2:15)

Each new infant carries the blood type of the father, including Jesus of Nazareth, the only begotten Son of God.

Those who abandon their inborn sexual identity sacrifice their ability to become biological parents. They have rejected God's most profound gift—the ability to participate in the creation of life <u>made in the image of God</u>—and His first instruction:

> *"Be fruitful and increase in number; fill the earth and subdue it."* (Genesis 1:28)

Not one of us is entitled or competent to judge another person's behavior or decision in this area. Drop it now, or you will be calling judgment onto yourself. Jesus says in Matt. 7:1–3: *"Do not judge, or you too will be judged. For in the same way you judge others, you will be judged, and with the measure you use, it will be measured to you."* God does not appoint anyone to force others to conform to his own convictions. In Matthew 19:12, Jesus says, *"For there are eunuchs who were born that way, and there are eunuchs who have been made eunuchs by others—and there are those who choose to live like eunuchs for the sake of the kingdom of heaven. The one who can accept this should accept it."* Look at Isaiah 56:3-5, also:

> *And let no eunuch complain,*
> *"I am only a dry tree."*
> *For this is what the Lord says:*

> *"To the eunuchs who keep my Sabbaths,*
> *who choose what pleases me*
> *and hold fast to my covenant—*
> *to them I will give within my temple and its walls*
> *a memorial and a name*
> *better than sons and daughters;*
> *I will give them an everlasting name*
> *that will endure forever.*

Society pays a steep price when children are no longer being raised by parents in a stable, healthy home. In our own nation, behaviors once considered horrifying, even psychotic, have become acceptable. People say, "Well, it's just human nature." Well, yes, it is human, and it is sinful. Our own sin—now viewed as normality—has made it almost impossible for a family to share life together for the long term, which would ensure that the children are guided safely into maturity with both parents engaged in their daily lives.

Jesus told the Pharisees that God allowed divorce because men's hearts were hard.

In our sick society, sick families abound, where neither parents nor children are safe. Some parents convince themselves that killing their unborn child is the best option. (Another customary practice that Satan enthusiastically promotes.) The books of the Original Testament describe the custom of delivering babies into the fire of Molech. Why? Why would parents *ever* do this? So that the crops would flourish. To stave off drought and famine. To gain acceptance into a more desirable peer group. In fact, it is the same motivation that parents have now: hope of increased wealth and prosperity, better life in the future, affirmation in the community, or whatever reason; it is a selfish delusion, and God holds fathers responsible.

The only weapon Satan has is to make you believe something that is not true.

Our own personal sin creates the opportunity for deception, and we are all too eager to persuade ourselves that the "something horrible" in our own heart is actually quite understandable.

This is now the third decade of the second millenia since the birth in the stable, and the effects of the Digital Age on the human family are not yet established. The supernatural state of being "in love"—a "God thing" if there ever was one—still ignites the desire to start a family, an indication that the human family will soon expand and acquire one more. The next phase of male/female life together is shared sexual enjoyment, leading to the conception of a new human being, made in the image of God. These life phases are still operational, even though heterosexual monogamy is no longer recognized as the mainstay of human society.

Even now, in the Digital Age, no one can adequately describe the effect a newborn has on the parents meeting him for the first time. The combined genetic material of the parents has miraculously produced a new one-of-a-kind human, bone of their bone and flesh of their flesh. Parents, still in love with each other, now experience the magnification of that shared love beyond all imagination, when their infant makes his appearance. The new mom and dad can be heard whispering ecstatically, "Look at her! She is *ours*!"

This overwhelming, unreasonable love is the destiny that our heavenly Father has always planned for humankind. Jesus said that we must become like little children to enter the kingdom of God. Angels rejoice over every newborn in God's family, a person who has repented and joined the family of believers. <u>This is the meaning of life</u>.

On the material/natural side, after the infant's birth, supporting the family becomes the number one priority for each member. All endeavors serve that end. Career becomes a means of ensuring the family's stability rather than a path to self-fulfillment or personal wealth. Historically, parents have put aside their own cherished dreams in order to provide an appropriate home for their children. Protecting the family has been the culturally approved supreme objective of every decision, at least until recently, when wealth and technology have made it much easier to get through life without it.

God created us in His own image because He wanted children, not employees or committee members. He wanted to be a father. Each of us, by a decision of our own free will, can become a partaker of His divine nature, capable of divine companionship, a child who "really takes after his father." Each human is a particular expression of God's infinite creativity. Not only is each person absolutely individual, but our Creator also knows each of us absolutely. He not only created us; He loves each person in an absolutely individual way, far beyond the grasp of human intellect.

Family is what life is about. **God created us because He wanted to have a family**. In a healthy family, biological grandparents, aunts, uncles, and cousins become the intrinsic components of lifelong fun, shared memories, love and support in hard times, sustaining permanent relationships of incalculable value, all of which is enhanced by shared DNA. That is God's design and His purpose for humanity. He created us specifically to experience that overwhelming, eternal, familial love with Him. I am His child. He made me. I am the only me He will ever have.

The meaning of life is discovered in the love inspired by parenthood and realized in the creation of a new family.

A personal anecdote:

At a friend's house for dinner, I met a woman who was at that time the manager of a fertility clinic in a large urban environment. During our conversation, she fervently expressed to me her serious concern that people don't really understand the ramifications of parenting a child who does not share their, as she put it, genetic material. She told me that she made a point to emphasize to each client that they really should not take this lightly. But, although the biological family is inarguably the best-case scenario for family life, God can redeem any situation.

CHAPTER 6
Forgotten Enemy

He was a murderer from the beginning, not holding to the truth, for there is no truth in him. When he lies, he speaks his native language, for he is a liar and the father of lies.
—John 8:44

We have a clever and subtle enemy, known as the devil, Satan, and "that old serpent," with a few other labels as well. Satan is proficient at muddying religious waters and substituting debates about doctrines and traditions for speaking the truth in love. Reiterated several times already, his only weapon is deception, enticing us into believing something that's not true. He is a liar and the father of lies. He expertly orchestrates a demonic conspiracy that has been active in human society since Adam and Eve made their fatal error in the garden of Eden.

He was a murderer from the beginning, not holding to the truth, for there is no truth in him. When he

> *lies, he speaks his native language, for he is a liar and the father of lies.* (John 8:44)

> *Now the serpent was more crafty than any of the wild animals the Lord God had made. He said to the woman, "Did God really say, 'You must not eat from any tree in the garden'?"* (Gen. 3:1)

The word *serpent* denotes Satan. Revelation 12:9 clarifies the identity of this creature, in case there's any confusion:

> *The great dragon was hurled down—that ancient serpent called the devil, or Satan, who leads the whole world astray.*

At the beginning of human history, two trees in the garden of Eden were enough to expose the danger of endowing humans with free will. The fruit of the tree of the knowledge of good and evil had been forbidden by God; the tree of life had not. Many volumes over many centuries have documented man's intellectual struggle with this situation. Satan asked Eve a question: "Did God really say...?"

Our enemy always uses the same strategy: persuading you that something false is true.

Every temptation to turn from God is always based on this one question: "Did God really say...?"

> *The woman said to the serpent, "We may eat fruit from the trees in the garden, but God did say, 'You must not eat fruit from the tree that is in the middle of the garden, and you must not touch it, or you will die.'"* (Gen. 3:2–3)

Notice that Eve misstated the Creator's command. God had not said not to touch the tree, only not to eat its fruit. Eve had stepped outside the boundary of truth into the domain of the deceiver.

Our adversary, Satan (a.k.a. devil, dragon, and/or serpent), cannot create anything, and he cannot destroy anything God has made. He does, however, have one disturbingly effective weapon that he wields with skill, cunning, and ruthlessness. He is a liar and the father of lies. He understands the inner consciousness of man, where secret desires are coddled, where each person is wanting to be convinced that something coveted is, in fact, deserved. The devil does not know your thoughts as your heavenly Father does, but he can easily determine your weaknesses from your speech and behavior. He uses your secret desires to uncover what kind of deception you are likely to accept. He convinces you that something false is true, then he does his best to ruin you and use you to ruin others.

Although the devil can't read your thoughts, he is certainly trying continually to influence them. He is, for now, the ruler of this world and the prince of the power of the air. The cartoon of a little demon on your shoulder whispering in your ear is actually not totally inaccurate; your actions let him know if his tactics are succeeding. He'll take as much as you allow him to have.

> *"You will not certainly die," the serpent said to the woman. "For God knows that when you eat from it your eyes will be opened, and you will be like God, knowing good and evil." When the woman saw that the fruit of the tree was good for food and pleasing to the eye, and also desirable for gaining wisdom, she took some and ate it. She also gave some to her husband, who was with her, and he ate it. Then the eyes of both of them were opened, and they realized they were naked; so they sewed fig leaves together and made coverings for themselves.* (Gen. 3:4–7)

Ancient folklore from diverse cultures attributes speech to dragons; the voice of a dragon is said to have hypnotic power, causing the listener to become enchanted and lose his free will. It's easy to see how that idea could have its origin in the *Genesis* story. In recent years, the popularity of mythology and fantasy in literature, movies, television series, video games, and social media has given dragon lore a prominent position in popular culture.

In fact, a modern speech recognition software company has chosen Dragon as a brand name, and there's now a civilian space shuttle with the same name, which is interesting, since the Bible tells us that the devil is the prince of the power of the air.

> *So the Lord God said to the serpent, "Because you have done this, "Cursed are you above all livestock and all wild animals! You will crawl on your belly and you will eat dust all the days of your life. And I will put enmity between you and the woman, and between your offspring and hers; he will crush your head, and you will strike his heel."* (Gen. 3:14–15)

This is the protoevangelium, the first prophetic promise of the coming Messiah, the Christ, the Anointed One, who defeats Satan, the father of lies, and saves man from deception. The woman's offspring is singled out, foreshadowing the virgin birth of the Messiah. The serpent will be crushed while striking the heel of the Anointed One.

Adam and Eve had no idea there was any such thing as good or evil and would have had no need of this knowledge as long as they continued in communion with God. Being made in His image, and tending to work that He had given them, nothing would have disturbed the fellowship they enjoyed together in their wonderful habitat. God had made it pleasing to their eyes; He created beauty especially for them. That fruit was lovely (Eve could see that it was beautiful) and tasty (nothing in Eden was not tasty), and supposedly good brain food.

When that delicious morsel entered their digestive systems, something happened; perhaps the first DNA mutation began with the introduction of this substance into their bodies. Decay and death were activated, and since the humans had been designated by God caretakers of the planet, nature, being under human authority, also suffered, and still suffers, the consequences of their action.

> *To the woman he said, "I will make your pains in childbearing very severe; with painful labor you will give birth to children. Your desire will be for your husband, and he will rule over you."* (Gen. 3:16)

The truth of this statement is evident and borne out by history. Eve compromised her equality with Adam by influencing him to disobey God, and women continue to pay the price, striving to please their mates even while suffering oppression.

One of Satan's major schemes is to corrupt the intended meaning of a verbal remark while it is in transit from one person to another through the atmosphere that is his bailiwick. Neither person is aware of the confusion until later, when the misunderstanding results in something bad—sometimes very bad, seriously injurious—happening. Sin in the listener, such as jealousy or anger, predisposes him to internalize the "mangled" remark without sufficient scrutiny. This happens regularly in groups of people, whatever the purpose of the gathering. Bible teachers are particularly susceptible to misinterpretation and must acquire some skills to try to prevent it.

At Babel, God confused the language; the spoken words did not have to be modified for this to take place. All that had to happen was that each person's self-concept be disrupted, possibly by some embarrassing personal distress, causing him to misinterpret the words he heard and preventing him from receiving whatever message the speaker intended. One can easily imagine everyone involved in the construction process getting seriously offended over imagined insults or dangerously misconstruing project specifications, both of which happen every day wherever people are trying to collaborate. Each person is enslaved to his own intimate interpretations but unable to recognize it as bondage.

When accurately judging truth and falsehood becomes impossible, Satan's subtle trickery has established open season. (This is not the only time that God uses Satan to help Him achieve His objective.) All information is now distorted by self-concept. Personal fulfillment has become a mirage, built on the shifting sand of deceptive psychological self-actualization and the frantic quest for peer affirmation. From this point forward, the global human community is broken, and the diverging cultures develop distinct languages. Humans require language in order to think, and a person's ability to process information is tied to his fluency with language. A person's native language, as manifested in its vocalization, grammatical structure, and use of idioms, determines to a large degree how he sees the world around him. For example, a Japanese person will interpret a scenario or solve a problem differently than a Spaniard, both of whom will differ from a Nigerian. American English and British English lend themselves to different frames of mind, as is clear by what each considers humorous. Language imposes boundaries on human cognition, effectively limiting an individual's personal comprehension.

> *"God gave them a spirit of stupor, eyes that could not see and ears that could not hear, to this very day,"* (Rom. 11:8)

> *See, darkness covers the earth and thick darkness is over the peoples.* (Isa. 60:2)

The darkness that blankets the lost contrasts sharply with the Light that shines over those who have surrendered to God:

> *But the* LORD *rises upon you and his glory appears over you.* (Isa. 60:2)

Analyses of Satan's motivation are prolific: jealous hatred of man for whatever reason, rage toward God, rooted in ambitious power-seeking; and others. Why he is the way he is, or does the things he does, is not relevant; he will never respond to remedial counseling. Isaiah chapter 14 and Ezekiel chapter 28 offer some insight into the nature of this formerly formidable creature who has chosen to hate what is good and corrupt what is innocent. We would certainly be in a much worse situation if the serpent had been the "god of the Old Testament," which, evidently, was the position he coveted.

Note:

Have you been in a middle school hallway during class change recently? Do you know how students are treated by their "peers" for being good or innocent? Disturbing, once unthinkable, never imagined (except by the enemy) is now customary. Right now. Ignoring the reality of a child's sinful desires does not help him overcome them or save him from them. Behaving as if evil doesn't exist does not protect children from it. Quite the opposite—it makes them more vulnerable. Believing he doesn't exist is the very best thing we can do to help Satan succeed.

The devil is not a fair fighter. He is ruthless and cruel. He incited Pharaoh to order the midwives to kill every male Hebrew at birth. He prompted Herod to order the massacre of all boys in Bethlehem who were two years old and under. He has coaxed generations of genteel churchgoers, the epitome of good Christians, to become comfortable with the notion that dark-skinned people are subhuman. He convinced Hitler that exterminating the entire population of Jews in Europe was the right thing to do. We live in a culture now that applauds the legal murder of unborn infants, numbering 629,898 in the US in 2019.

Satan gleefully receives the worship of ignorant adolescents (ignorant because the adults in their lives have sanctioned and enforced their ignorance) who are trying to be "cool" and persuades them to commit deeds, including mass murder, that will stain them and their families forever. This cruel taskmaster does not wait to be worshiped, though, to induce nightmarish behavior in schoolchildren that as little as fifty years ago was inconceivable. The Columbine shooting that opened the floodgates of deadly school violence occurred in 1999.

The devil is eager to utilize any human vulnerability to achieve his purpose, which is to take as many humans as possible into hell with him at the last judgment. We are told that he is filled with rage because he knows his time is short.

To be clear: murdered infants do not go to hell with the devil. The adults, however, who approve, plan, support, pay for, work toward, deliberately ignore, and commit these murders will certainly answer for it. The devil will enjoy the show as long as he can.

It is your own unconfessed sin that gives Satan power over you. An individual cannot even identify his own sin until God reveals it, at which time it suddenly becomes sickeningly garish and inescapable. Confessing your sin, agreeing with God, allows Him to come in and do warfare on your behalf.

The only thing God requires of you is honesty.

CHAPTER 7

Forsaken Salvation

Continue to work out your salvation with fear and trembling.
—Phil. 2:12

Though you have not seen him, you love him; and even though you do not see him now, you believe in him and are filled with an inexpressible and glorious joy, for you are receiving the end result of your faith, the salvation of your souls.
—1 Pet. 1:8–9

At their point of disobedience, Adam and Eve rejected the authority of the spirit that God had breathed into them and His voice that spoke to them. Instead, they opted for the "knowledge of good and evil," transferring guidance for their decisions and behavior to their own souls—in other words, mind, will, and emotions. From then on, their communication and relationship with the Creator would be defined by their limited intellects and unreliable feelings rather than by His spirit within them. Self-inflicted imprisonment had begun.

Self-awareness came first; then self-consciousness and self-interest. The first revelation was that they were naked and that being naked was somehow uncomfortable. Nothing left to the imagination; vulnerable, devoid of protection; everything out in the open; no privacy; defenseless; transparent; nothing hidden; the honest truth—they were mortified. They hurried to cover themselves with aprons made of fig leaves. The first decision using the new ability to discern right and wrong was to decide being naked was wrong. (Throughout the Bible, the fig tree signifies human judgment; in Hebrew tradition, the fig was associated with the Sanhedrin. More about this elsewhere.)

> *Then the man and his wife heard the sound of the Lord God as he was walking in the garden in the cool of the day, and they hid from the Lord God among the trees of the garden. But the Lord God called to the man, "Where are you?"* (Gen. 3:8–9)

As has been ruefully recognized by believers everywhere, when the Creator asks you a question, it isn't because He doesn't know the answer. Tragically, the first emotion triggered by Adam and Eve's disobedience was shame; they had discovered "the God of the Old Testament."

> *He answered, "I heard you in the garden, and I was afraid because I was naked; so I hid."* (Gen. 3:10)

Adam did not stand to face the Light and be questioned, as Job did; he hid. The first step in the manufacture of a personal identity outside God's presence had been taken. Truth, light, reality, and eternity had been chucked overboard.

> *And he said, "Who told you that you were naked? Have you eaten from the tree that I commanded you not to eat from?" The man said, "The woman you put here with me—she gave me some fruit from the tree, and I ate it." Then the Lord God said to the*

> *woman, "What is this you have done?" The woman said, "The serpent deceived me, and I ate." (Gen. 3:11–12)*

This story is so pitifully human! Self-aware, self-conscious, ashamed when forced to face facts, what do we do? Become self-righteous. Prevaricate. Put up a barrier. Make an excuse. Present a defense. Rationalize. Blame someone else. We are very, very good at this, remarkably adept at deceiving ourselves most of all. Today this internal, highly personal process is called creating my own truth, discovering my identity, finding the real me, reinventing myself, or some such. It is self-deception, pure and simple.

Once the decision was made to disagree with and disobey the Creator, the floodgates were opened, and human history has ever since been a maelstrom of fervent, even desperate, human self-interest. This is why Jesus told Nicodemus in John chapter 3 that we must be born again by the Spirit of God; until that happens, we are in bondage to our own psyches, ignorant of the truth.

At its root, this psychological persona, so intricately constructed and painstakingly maintained, is nothing more than self-deception, and that, my friends, is sin. It means we depend on our intellects to define right and wrong, good and evil. It separates us from our heavenly Father, and we cannot even perceive it, much less extricate ourselves from it, without supernatural help.

Salvation does not mean escaping hell and going to heaven when you die. That's like telling a teenager that when he gets his driver's license, he'll be allowed to park the car in the garage. In fact, salvation has hardly anything to do with biological life and death at all.

The Bible says that the heart of man is desperately wicked. Our need for salvation is in our inner man (also known as heart, spirit, persona, psyche, schema), where each of us is bound up in a self-made cocoon of deception with no hope for escape. It's a dense web, woven of numberless threads that are individually almost invisible, wrapping us in a continually constricting death trap that we have been convinced is our only place of safety. Our complex, carefully fabricated and maintained persona is what we use to justify, rationalize, conceal, and cope. It houses the continually looping secret voice that expresses what we hide from the world and ourselves.

Self-centeredness is not openly admired in our culture, so consequently, much of our ego is kept busy figuring out ways to convince everyone (especially our own self) that what we do is always for someone else's benefit. This is tricky. The real reason we help out at the homeless shelter is because we value being admired for our charity. We go to church faithfully because it's required for acceptance—though no one one would ever say so—in the pillar-of-the-community club. Our grandchildren really enjoy the boat, and so forth. Our intellects are mostly occupied with shoring up our cherished but fragile realities. We have blind spots and biases. All of this is pervasive in human society, but the fact is, we are continually inventing more lies to cover it up or explain it away. To our own selves. A house of cards.

The sin nature is the human persona's desperate attempt to forge a meaningful identity, process information, cope with life experiences, and maintain psychological equilibrium, while avoiding the truth and staying out of the light. <u>Sin is not what we do; it is what we are.</u> Of course, who I am determines the decisions and choices I make, the words I speak, the actions I take, and the behavior I exhibit, but correcting these things—like quitting smoking—will not undo who I am. It is impossible to reject, ignore, or bypass your personal schema to discern reality without the supernatural assistance of the Holy Spirit. The sin nature is the most secret of secret places of the heart, and we need to be saved from it. We need to be rescued from our own lies and the blindness that makes it impossible for us to even see them.

Some say that people use religion as a crutch. Well, the first thing Jesus starts doing in your heart, after you invite Him in, is knocking your crutches out from under you. Your personal dishonesties are the first things that start getting jettisoned when you set out on your journey to know the Creator. This is hard—we want so very much for those things to be true, and everyone has been telling us all our lives that we make our own truth and can achieve anything we want to, if only we try hard enough.

You may have actually convinced yourself, along with a few good friends, that the persona you have been projecting (or parts of it, anyway) is your true self. However, the reality might be that we only befriend those who believe and help us maintain our dishonesties. If other people believe it, that makes it true, right?

Your heavenly Father is not at all concerned about totally crushing the false "self-esteem" you've been working so hard to construct. But when you come to your senses and agree with Him, He is merciful and kind, and rewards your smallest efforts with overwhelming loving-kindness; like the prodigal son—his father saw him coming from a long way off and ran to meet him. As previously stated, **The only thing God requires from us is honesty.**

Simple, but not easy. Our loving Father does everything else: reveals our sin to us, enables us to repent, gives us the willingness and the ability to obey. He imparts His divine nature to us.

Honesty is extraordinarily difficult for people to achieve. From conception, every one of us is receiving and processing information in a highly individualized manner. Every detail is absorbed, evaluated, categorized, and added to the continually expanding persona that we never stop constructing during our existence on this planet. Some might call this the subconscious. Educators call this internal psychological structure the schema, and its development, education. Poet Gerard Manley Hopkins called it the inscape, and the incorporation of new information he called instress. As one of his poems states:

> *Oh, the Mind, mind has mountains*
> *Cliffs of fall, frightful, sheer, no-man-fathomed*

The gospel is not about political action, or social justice, or self-actualization. According to the texts of the New Testament, Jesus gave no attention at all to the brutal oppression of the Roman Empire, the evils of slavery, the debauchery of pagan religion, or even its customary pedophilia. He didn't give an inspiring sermon and then say, "Now, get out there and shut down those brothels." His teaching was not about saving the world, but about saving your soul. If you can grasp it, it's about being reborn as a different species of human.

An individual accepting eternal life from the Lord Jesus Christ is born again—literally—into a different dimension, the eternal kingdom of God, remaining physically in the world, but no longer a native of the world. Biological death is not necessary to experience eternal life. You can be lifted out of your self-imposed delusion and become aware of your self-imposed incarceration, your internal house of cards. This is being convicted of your sin. This is the supernatural help you need; you can no longer hide from your personal dishonesties. Instead, you can confess and be liberated from deception. That's what repentence and salvation means.

Eternal life is not learned or earned.

You shall know the truth, and the truth shall set you free. Starting now.

A common concern that often pops up here is, if the cocooned psyche inside the house of cards in my heart is not the real me, then who the heck am I?

Now begins the incredible adventure of learning who God created you to be.

The Bible often exhorts us to be not hearers only, but doers of the Word. James 1:22 warns that those who hear the Word but do not put it into practice deceive themselves, merely throwing another veil over the heart. Our supernatural help is enacted when we determine to obey the Lord and put His word into practice. In the parable of the wise and foolish builders in Matthew chapter 7, Jesus emphasizes the consequences of hearing but not doing:

> *"Therefore everyone who hears these words of mine and puts them into practice is like a wise man who built his house on the rock. The rain came down, the streams rose, and the winds blew and beat against that house; yet it did not fall, because it had its foundation on the rock. But everyone who hears*

> *these words of mine and does not put them into practice is like a foolish man who built his house on sand. The rain came down, the streams rose, and the winds blew and beat against that house, and it fell with a great crash."* (Matt. 7:24–27)

This is where the rubber meets the road, as they say. Putting His word into practice requires outright deliberate rejection of the comfortable but blinding personal schema, which is another of those decisions that may be simple, but not easy. In this situation also, **<u>the decision to obey comes first</u>**. It entails nothing less than putting to death your self, your most precious false identity, your hard-won self-esteem, and allowing the Holy Spirit to rule.

> *I have been executed with Christ and I no longer live, but Christ lives in me. The life I now live in the body, I live by faith in the Son of God, who loved me and gave himself for me.* (Gal. 2:20)

> *I want to know Christ—yes, to know the power of his resurrection and participation in his sufferings, becoming like him in his death, and so, somehow, attaining to the resurrection from the dead.* (Phil. 3:10–11)

Because every person is created in the image of God, every word he uses has an indelible effect on the atmosphere; it can never be unsaid, and most of its consequences are unforeseen and unintended. Making the choice to walk in the Light gives the believer the ability to change his environment consciously and deliberately, by rejecting the world's wisdom, which is exhibited by the sin nature, and choosing obedience to God's Word, which means returning good for evil, blessing instead of cursing, and praying for your enemies.

> "But as many as received him, to them gave he <u>power to become the sons of God</u>, even to them that believe on his name." (John 1:12)

> *Consider it pure joy, my brothers and sisters, whenever you face trials of many kinds, because you know that the testing of your faith produces perseverance. Let perseverance finish its work so that you may be mature and complete, not lacking anything. If any of you lacks wisdom, you should ask God, who gives generously to all without finding fault, and it will be given to you. But when you ask, you must believe and not doubt, because the one who doubts is like a wave of the sea, blown and tossed by the wind. That person should not expect to receive anything from the Lord. Such a person is double-minded and unstable in all they do.* (James 1:2–8)

An honest heart seeking to know God will hear Him. He speaks to each of us in the secret language of our inner man that only He understands.

> *"You will seek me and find me when you seek me with all your heart. I will be found by you," declares the Lord.* (Jer. 29:13–14)

When you ask God for wisdom, He will grant it. It will be something that you would never have thought of yourself. It will require courage; otherwise, it's not a real adventure. Take a deep breath, and go for it. You will be amazed. (It is just SO COOL.) Don't worry. If you are sincerely focused on obeying Him, He can correct any misstep you make. Remember, **<u>the one thing you can't do is try it out just to see if it works</u>**.

The concept of choosing words, controlling our conversation, is a foundational element of the Bible. Praise brings God's presence (Ps.

22:3) and repulses our accuser, the devil. Blessing instead of cursing our earthly enemies (Rom. 12:14; Matt. 5:44; Luke 6:28) establishes our position as God's children, turning back any curse headed our way, putting us outside the influence of the deceiver. Thanks in every situation (1 Thess. 5:18) indicates to all heavenly powers that we are fulfilling the eternal destiny our heavenly Father created for us.

> *Those who consider themselves religious and yet do not keep a tight rein on their tongues deceive themselves, and their <u>religion is worthless.</u>* (James 1:26)

When those daily opportunities arise to implement this word power, though, things don't seem so clear and simple. Taking every thought captive and controlling each spoken word require constant diligent attention, possible only with the supernatural help of the Holy Spirit. We always retain the ability to choose, and we rout the enemy by filling our atmosphere—our own personal space—with praise and thanksgiving.

> *Therefore, my beloved, as you have always obeyed, not as in my presence only, but now much more in my absence, <u>work out your own salvation with fear and trembling</u>; for it is God who works in you both to will and to do for His good pleasure.* (Phil. 2:12–13)

Confronting negative thoughts and replacing them with praise, blessing, and thanksgiving is a lifelong mental discipline, involving continual stumbling and trying again. We are constantly confronted with a sort of internal tape recorder (Who even knows what a tape recorder is anymore? Let's make it an audio file.) or audio file playing negative thoughts over and over on a loop, thoughts that are practically impossible to put into words because they are so personal. Satan tempts you to believe these thoughts are your own, that they are accurate, and that you are despised or mocked, being sinned against, or being taken advantage of in some serious way. He uses this strategy to drive a wedge between spouses in particular.

First, you have to recognize these thoughts and remember where they originate. Then, you make the choice to begin speaking aloud true, positive comments rather than complaints. When the eternal loop starts up again, seeking to establish itself in your heart, you react by immediately praising God, consciously and deliberately taking every thought captive, filling your sphere with the presence of the Creator. Even reciting Bible verses from memory helps. You will experience firsthand the power that comes from obeying God's word—which cannot be articulated using human language—and that blessing is multiplied when others in your community receive it from your presence. When you manifest the fruit of the Spirit in your daily life, others are nourished by it, even though they may be totally unaware. (More about that elsewhere).

The devil cannot be successful in your heart when you are focused on praising God. The Bible says that God inhabits the praises of His people; vocal praise and worship—meaning out loud—establishes God's presence in your sphere of influence. However, allowing only blessing and praise to come from your mouth requires the conscientious acquisition of new habits and constant practice. Controlling one's thoughts demands personal, long-term, continual discipline. <u>Spiritual warfare is conducted in the inner man, and that is where Satan is defeated</u>. Not at the ballot box or in a church sanctuary, in a classroom or on a battlefield. Not on another planet in another galaxy. Or, for that matter, in a test tube or a robot. This conflict is not being waged to correct cultural injustice but to rescue individual human beings. First of all, yourself.

If you're at a committee meeting or giving a presentation or something, you can worship God in silence, even then calming a situation of escalating confrontation. The devil may not be hearing your thoughts, but he will certainly realize that there is a disturbance in the force.

> *In all this you greatly rejoice, though now for a little while you may have had to suffer grief in all kinds of*

> *trials. These have come so that the proven genuineness of your faith—of greater worth than gold, which perishes even though refined by fire—may result in praise, glory and honor when Jesus Christ is revealed. Though you have not seen him, you love him; and even though you do not see him now, you believe in him and are filled with an inexpressible and glorious joy, for <u>you are receiving the end result of your faith, the salvation of your souls.</u>* (1 Pet. 1:6–9)

> *For though we walk in the flesh, we do not war after the flesh: For the weapons of our warfare are not carnal, but mighty through God to the pulling down of strongholds; Casting down imaginations, and every high thing that exalteth itself against the knowledge of God, and <u>bringing into captivity every thought to the obedience of Christ.</u>* (2 Cor. 10:3–5)

When a person's soul is saved, his mind, will, and emotions are brought under the authority of the Holy Spirit, while anxiety, confusion, and self-consciousness lose their grip. The fruit of the Spirit begins to appear, and he acquires the ability to be the master of his circumstances, not the victim. This means being proactive, not reactive; the controller, not the controlled. Attitude, speech, and behavior are no longer instigated by others' actions or the physical environment.

The blood of Jesus (Such a simple phrase! Treated by some as a useful catchphrase—God have mercy on us all) has paid the penalty for rebellion against God, and His resurrection manifests the supremacy of eternal life. When He ascended, He provided the Holy Spirit to be our constant companion, equipping us to re-establish dominion over the habitat that Adam had ceded to the enemy. Submission to the Holy Spirit enables the believer to bring the fruit of the Spirit into every situation. Some have said that believers can be distinguished from unbelievers because they speak different languages: believers praise; unbelievers complain.

> *"I am the vine; you are the branches. If you remain in me and I in you, you will bear much fruit; apart from me you can do nothing."* (John 15:5)

(I urge you to go read this whole chapter.)

> *But the fruit of the Spirit is love, joy, peace, forbearance, kindness, goodness, faithfulness, gentleness and self-control. Against such things there is no law.*
> (Gal. 5:22–23)

> *Bless those who persecute you; bless and do not curse.* (Rom. 12:14)

> *But I tell you, love your enemies and pray for those who persecute you, that you may be children of your Father in heaven. He causes his sun to rise on the evil and the good, and sends rain on the righteous and the unrighteous.* (Matt. 5:44–45)

> *But love your enemies, do good to them, and lend to them without expecting to get anything back. Then your reward will be great, and you will be children of the Most High, because he is kind to the ungrateful and wicked.* (Luke 6:35)

Jesus explained that He is the vine, and we are the branches; to bear fruit, we must abide in Him. The definition of that metaphor is found in the book of Galatians: the fruit of the Spirit is love, joy, peace, patience, kindness, goodness, gentleness, faithfulness, and self-control. We produce fruit as a result of abiding in Him, but not because we are striving to bear fruit. What vine concentrates on squeezing fruit out of its extremities? No—we just abide, and the fruit appears as a consequence of the nourishment we are receiving. This is what we have that nourishes the people around us.

Jesus also told His disciples that they would be His witnesses, not that they would go witness to others. We <u>are</u> His witnesses, 24/7/365. We just are. Our whole being, every moment of every day, is demonstrating how faithfully we are abiding in Him. Witnessing means that wherever we go, whoever we encounter is able to draw nourishment from us, usually without even realizing it. Our heavenly Father is pleased to bless every person, whether they thank Him or not. He is pleased to use us to make someone's day better. He doesn't want people to suffer, and if they won't come to Him for relief, He will use us to bless them in a way they can receive it.

Jesus reminded His disciples of the power that God originally intended man to wield as His steward over creation:

> *"Truly I tell you, if you have faith as small as a mustard seed, you can say to this mountain, 'Move from here to there,' and it will move. Nothing will be impossible for you."* (Matt. 17:20)

This verse is often translated in a way that implies faith the same size as a mustard seed, but a more accurate rendering might be the same amount of faith that a mustard seed has. What power we have, if only we agree with God; He intends that nothing be impossible for us! The conscious decision to surrender to God, saying yes to your Maker, recognizing who He is and who you are, brings the new birth and opens the door to eternal life.

The result of honesty is always humility.

Stepping into His light bestows upon the believer the power to become a child of God, to realize true and eternal purpose in life, and to be sustained by the personal teaching, counsel, and comfort of the Holy Spirit. Saying yes to the Creator and being born of the Spirit endow each person with the ability to escape the bondage of self and to walk in the light, as He is in the light. Only after being born by the Spirit is a person capable of making decisions outside the influence of his inner persona. The sacrificial death of the prophesied Christ made this possible.

Spiritual conflict occurs in a person's inner man, and victory occurs when the individual takes control of his own sphere of influence.

> *For our struggle is not against flesh and blood, but against the rulers, against the authorities, against the powers of this dark world and against the spiritual forces of evil in the heavenly realms.* (Eph. 6:12)

There is no political solution for spiritual problems. Endeavoring to correct systemic social injustice does not eliminate the need for individual personal repentence before God. In fact, individual repentance is what inspires and enables authentic "grassroots" social change.

Spiritual warfare, on both sides of the conflict, is totally waged within the individual human heart. Jesus's "Sermon on the Mount," found in the book of *Matthew*, is entirely focused on each person's responsibility for his own behavior. The objective of the Beatitudes is not removing corruption from civic organizations or correcting ungodly government policies, but instead recognising what qualities cause someone to be blessed. Unfortunately, this is not what denominational Christianity practices. In Matthew chapter 6, Jesus says:

> *"Be careful not to practice your righteousness in front of others to be seen by them. If you do, you will have no reward from your Father in heaven. So when you give to the needy, do not announce it with trumpets, as the hypocrites do in the synagogues and on the streets, to be honored by others. Truly I tell you, they have received their reward in full. But when you give to the needy, do not let your left hand know what your right hand is doing, so that your giving may be in secret. Then your Father, who sees what is done in secret, will reward you."* (Matt. 6:1–3)

American churchgoers are goal-driven and work-oriented, a legacy from our Puritan background. We like to do things that we can check off a list and get visible results, things that can be counted. We think of spiritual fruit in terms of numbers: people responding to altar calls, food baskets delivered, orphanages maintained, mission trips taken. Success is good numbers.

On the other hand, the fruit produced by abiding in the vine is manifested in words and deeds. Each of us inhabits a personal sphere of influence, which can be illustrated by common helping verbs: things we can do (ability), may do (authority), should do (ethics), and will do (choice). Each of us answers to God—no one else—for effective stewardship of our sphere. Each person who is born again and walking in the Light has the duty, the responsibility, and the means to take ownership of his space. The ownership of your space is exhibited to the world by your behavior. The fruit of the spirit (love, joy, peace, patience, kindness, goodness, gentleness, faithfulness, self-control) is available for the well-being of everyone around you.

Return good for evil. Bless rather than curse. Pray for people who despise you. This is a believer's natural method of operations, advertising to everyone around you that even though you are in the world, you are not a native of it.

One common demonic strategy is to distract well-meaning believers into exhausting themselves in "charitable" endeavors, amassing good works, instead of doing what our Savior told us to do: seek God first, love our neighbor, return good for evil, pray for our enemies. Political and social activism does not, cannot, replace prayer and personal repentance; on the contrary, it often disables it. Assembling together once a week is meaningless, or even destructive, if the individuals in the congregation are not communing daily with their Redeemer. The church—that means the believer—is being defrauded of true power to change lives, which happens one person at a time.

A personal anecdote:

I was in the checkout line at a busy grocery store where a new cashier was learning how to use the manually operated cash register. (Yes, I am really, really old.) She was nervous and insecure, which caused her to make mistakes. Her hostile customers were not helping. A woman behind me, who I think may have been carrying a birthday cake, was complaining loudly, shifting impatiently from foot to foot, that she was late and had to get out of there. I knew that I had the authority and the responsibility to bring love and peace into the situation, not for my own personal equilibrium but for everyone else in the area. **God's blessings are never limited to those who recognize them.**

I remained calm, smiled at people, and when I got up to the cashier, I looked at her and said, "Wow, you are having a hard day. It's okay. Take a breath, I've got time." Tears welled up in her eyes. The woman behind me suddenly became strangely calm. The peace rolled out palpably, like ripples in a pond, across lines, counters, shelves, and aisles. The cashier recovered, rang me up (this was before debit cards) smoothly and efficiently, and the day progressed.

CHAPTER 8

Forsaken Church

1 Cor. 12:27 Now you are the body of Christ, and each one of you is part of it.

—1 Cor. 12:27

The word *church* actually means "assembly." What most Americans call "church" today is nothing like the first-century church. For one thing, back in the day, it was customary for each believer to participate in the assembly. They <u>wanted</u> to participate; they came into the room bursting with something to share. Sometimes the enthusiastic participation needed to be toned down a little bit, to give everyone a fair chance to contribute. They were <u>all</u> hearing from God.

Sitting in pews and listening to someone talk is not a worship service.

When money was collected in the first-century church, it went directly to the poor. It seems that no one even imagined buying real estate in order to build facilities. In fact, the believers were selling their properties to give the money to the apostles.

People in the first-century church who told lies (as it happens, about how much money they got from selling property) were known to drop dead without warning.

Those who were involved in questionable conduct were discussed publicly, in writing, and sometimes expelled.

They sang new songs every time they met. In the Bible, we are not just encouraged, but repeatedly instructed, to sing a new song (Ps. 33:3, Ps. 96:1, Ps. 98:1, Ps. 144:9, Ps. 149:1, Isa. 42:10, et al). Singing Bible verses with other believers is worship.

> *Instead, be filled with the Spirit, speaking to one another with psalms, hymns, and songs from the Spirit. Sing and make music from your heart to the Lord, always giving thanks to God the Father for everything, in the name of our Lord Jesus Christ.* (Eph. 5:18–20)

The newborn church was compelling.

Chapter 12 from 1 Corinthians describes what church should be like:

> *There are different kinds of gifts, but the same Spirit distributes them. There are different kinds of service, but the same Lord. There are different kinds of working, but in all of them and in everyone it is the same God at work.*
>
> *Now to each one the manifestation of the Spirit is given for the common good. To one there is given through the Spirit a message of wisdom, to another a message of knowledge by means of the same Spirit, to another faith by the same Spirit, to another gifts of healing by that one Spirit, to another miraculous powers, to another prophecy, to another distinguishing between spirits, to another speaking in different kinds of tongues, and to still another the interpretation of tongues. All these are the work of*

one and the same Spirit, and he distributes them to each one, just as he determines.

Just as a body, though one, has many parts, but all its many parts form one body, so it is with Christ. For we were all baptized by one Spirit so as to form one body—whether Jews or Gentiles, slave or free— and we were all given the one Spirit to drink. Even so the body is not made up of one part but of many.

Now if the foot should say, "Because I am not a hand, I do not belong to the body," it would not for that reason stop being part of the body. And if the ear should say, "Because I am not an eye, I do not belong to the body," it would not for that reason stop being part of the body. If the whole body were an eye, where would the sense of hearing be? If the whole body were an ear, where would the sense of smell be?

But in fact God has placed the parts in the body, every one of them, just as he wanted them to be. If they were all one part, where would the body be? As it is, there are many parts, but one body. The eye cannot say to the hand, "I don't need you!" And the head cannot say to the feet, "I don't need you!" On the contrary, those parts of the body that seem to be weaker are indispensable, and the parts that we think are less honorable we treat with special honor. And the parts that are unpresentable are treated with special modesty, while our presentable parts need no special treatment. But God has put the body together, giving greater honor to the parts that lacked it, so that there should be no division in the body, but that its parts should have equal concern for each other. If one part suffers, every part suffers with it; if one part is honored, every part rejoices with it.

> *Now you are the body of Christ, and each one of you is a part of it. And God has placed in the church first of all apostles, second prophets, third teachers, then miracles, then gifts of healing, of helping, of guidance, and of different kinds of tongues. Are all apostles? Are all prophets? Are all teachers? Do all work miracles? Do all have gifts of healing? Do all speak in tongue? Do all interpret? Now eagerly desire the greater gifts.* (1 Cor. 12)

Let me encourage you again to take your questions and concerns to your heavenly Father. He favors no other child ahead of you. He loves no other child more than He loves you. He wants you to be close to Him, just as close as anyone else. He wants you to know His voice. In fact, the reason that the Lord Jesus Christ submitted to the horrific punishment that He did is so that <u>you would belong in the presence of God.</u> The "body of Christ" is one of the Bible's transcendent metaphors, a spiritual fractal that is continually revealing unforeseen aspects of God's nature and attributes, His unchanging but always unexpected reality, expanding into infinity.

A living organism is far more complicated to manage than a corporation. The Holy Spirit, however, has no problem supervising the enthusiasm of eccentric characters who have been known to heal people by laying hands on them or by passing along a piece of advice that changed somebody's life; or when someone reads a chapter from the Bible and explains how God showed him why it is relevant right now; or when someone in the back begins singing a scripture song that no one else has ever heard, growing louder and louder until others start joining in and harmonizing, producing musical instruments seemingly out of nowhere, and dancing in the aisles; while at the same time, someone in the corridor is quietly slipping someone else a few hundred dollar bills because God told him to. Those kinds of assemblies can't be formatted into a consistent schedule, and truthfully, sometimes embarrassing things happen, and people get offended.

On the other hand, a bureaucratic hierarchy with a paid staff can guarantee a standard timetable for meetings and maintain a weekly schedule of events, such as a healing service every Thursday evening. It can provide some stable career options, where people can advance to a higher standard of living while earning the admiration of their peers, being accepted into the highest level of local powers-that-be. It provides important services to the community. Eternal life is addressed in a nonthreatening environment where no one is made to feel guilty (which, actually, is the one thing they <u>must</u> feel in order to move from darkness into light).

A bureaucratic hierarchy, however well-meaning at its inception, cannot replace or even coexist with a living body, any more than an athlete can compete while dependent on an iron lung for oxygen. The denominational model of religion that is still socially acceptable in the United States is possibly a useful, even beneficial, organization, but it is not Christianity. (The label "Christian" was first used to denote believers in Antioch because they could do the works that Christ did.) A bureaucratic hierarchy can't be healed or reorganized to establish its validity. In fact, it's a fraud, not serving the purpose it was ostensibly established for (being the supernatural body of Christ on earth as described in the Bible) but rather safeguarding its own structure.

That does not at all mean that the folks in the pews are participating in a con or that they are stupid. As already stated, every denomination includes individuals who know God and live to serve Him, participating in organized church programs that really help people. And some—but not nearly enough—American Christians are blessed to participate in a fellowship that does exemplify the body of Christ. And there are many churchgoers who remain faithful because it's what they know to do, to worship God. They've never even been exposed to the actual gospel.

Frankly, the American "church" is vegetating in a spiritual condition that, in order to function as the body of Christ, requires nothing less than shutting down, restarting, and rebooting. A real revival, not just a visiting preacher for a week. Embarrassing things must happen. Offended people should leave and go somewhere else.

It is not a good sign if you have defaulted to a defensive attitude about your church while reading these words. Of course, there are still congregations that really love God and care for each other, and every congregation probably has at least one true believer. But the familiar American denominational church stopped being the body of Christ a long time ago (if it ever was), choosing to function as a corporation rather than an unpredictable bunch of Jesus freaks. There aren't many miracles happening, but some people still donate money, most of which goes to sustain the corporate structure.

For the American denominational church, restarting means each individual believer taking responsibility for his own relationship with the Creator. This might require drastic measures, like personally going back to the Bible and approaching the text with the deliberate intention of finding out what God has to say and then deciding whether to agree or not rather than searching for proof texts to back up an opinion.

Each of us answers for our own communication with our heavenly Father, being His child first of all. We are supposed to participate in our assemblies so He can use each of us to bless the others. Each one of us needs to read His Word and hear His voice, because <u>He is the one who not only knows your secret language but also where you belong in His church.</u> Rebooting, once more submitting to the Holy Spirit's power, so that God Himself is working in us and through us. That's why He created us, so that we could be, as the Apostle Peter puts it, "partakers of the divine nature."

Here are some thought-provoking snippets from Paul's letters to Timothy, instructions to a pastor:

1 Timothy:

> *Yyou will know how people ought to conduct themselves in God's household, which is the church of the living God, the pillar and foundation of the truth.*
>
> *The Spirit clearly says that in later times some will abandon the faith and follow deceiving spirits*

and things taught by demons. Such teachings come through hypocritical liars, whose consciences have been seared as with a hot iron.

They forbid people to marry and order them to abstain from certain foods, which God created to be received with thanksgiving by those who believe and who know the truth.

If anyone teaches otherwise and does not agree to the sound instruction of our Lord Jesus Christ and to godly teaching, they are conceited and understand nothing.

They have an unhealthy interest in controversies and quarrels about words that result in envy, strife, malicious talk, evil suspicions, and constant friction between people of corrupt mind, who have been robbed of the truth and who think that godliness is a means to financial gain.

2 Timothy:

Do your best to present yourself to God as one approved, a worker who does not need to be ashamed and who correctly handles the word of truth.

Avoid godless chatter because those who indulge in it will become more and more ungodly.

Their teaching will spread like gangrene.

Among them are Hymenaeus and Philetus, who have departed from the truth. They say that the resurrection has already taken place, and they destroy the faith of some.

Opponents must be gently instructed, in the hope that God will grant them repentance leading them to a knowledge of the truth.

But mark this: There will be terrible times in the last days. People will be lovers of themselves, lovers of money, boastful, proud, abusive, disobedient to their parents, ungrateful, unholy, without love, unforgiving, slanderous, without self-control, brutal, not lovers of the good, treacherous, rash, conceited, lovers of pleasure rather than lovers of God—having a form of godliness but denying its power.

Have nothing to do with such people.

They are the kind who worm their way into homes and gain control over gullible women, who are loaded down with sins and are swayed by all kinds of evil desires, always learning but never able to come to a knowledge of the truth.

For the time will come when people will not put up with sound doctrine.

Instead, to suit their own desires, they will gather around them a great number of teachers to say what their itching ears want to hear.

They will turn their ears away from the truth and turn aside to myths.

So, what is the big deal? Isn't the local church an important part of the community, where people can find out that God loves them no matter what? Where everyone feels welcomed and included? Where teenagers can find safe, wholesome social activities? Where parents can find affordable and educational child care options?

Actually, no. None of the above.

God's purpose for His church is to use it to humiliate the devil.

> *His intent was that now, <u>through the church</u>, the manifold wisdom of God should be made known to the rulers and authorities in the heavenly realms, according to his eternal purpose that he accomplished in Christ Jesus our Lord.* (Eph. 3:10–11)

CHAPTER 9

Forsaken Redeemer

I know that my redeemer lives, and that in the end he will stand on the earth. And after my skin has been destroyed, yet in my flesh I will see God; I myself will see him with my own eyes—I, and not another.
—Job 19:25–27

The literal definition of *redeem* is to buy back. This term appears twice in *Exodus* (6:6, 15:13) and four times in *Deuteronomy* (15:15, 21:8, 24:18).

> *But it was because the Lord loved you and kept the oath he swore to your ancestors that he brought you out with a mighty hand and redeemed you from the land of slavery, from the power of Pharaoh king of Egypt.* (Deut. 7:8)
>
> *I know that my redeemer lives, and that in the end he will stand on the earth. And after my skin has*

> *been destroyed, yet in my flesh I will see God; I myself will see him with my own eyes—I, and not another. How my heart yearns within me!* (Job 19:25–27)

Does any other faith's scripture compare with *Job*'s literary power and beauty?

Redemption appears twelve times in *Psalms*, in various contexts. David used a psalm to pray for redemption twice (119:134, 119:154). He also speaks about Israel, as well as himself, being redeemed from death (49:15), the oppressor (78:42), from the pit (103:4), the hand of the enemy (106:10), the hand of the foe (107:2), and all sins (130:8). He called God the Redeemer of Israel three times (74:2, 78:35).

Note David's humble and affectionate tone in his personal communion with his Creator:

> *May these words of my mouth and this meditation of my heart be pleasing in your sight, Lord, my Rock and my Redeemer.* (Ps. 19:14)

Isaiah mentions redemption more than twenty times, more than can be investigated here. But look at this:

> *Do not be afraid, you worm* (<u>Crimson worm again!</u> More about this elsewhere.) *Jacob, little Israel, do not fear, for I myself will help you," declares the Lord, your Redeemer, the Holy One of Israel.* (Isa. 41:14)

Another insurpassable example of literary power and beauty:

> *"I have swept away your offenses like a cloud, your sins like the morning mist. Return to me, for I have redeemed you." Sing for joy, you heavens, for the Lord has done this; shout aloud, you earth beneath. Burst into song, you mountains, you forests and*

> *all your trees, for the Lord has redeemed Jacob, he displays his glory in Israel.*
>
> *"This is what the Lord says—your Redeemer, who formed you in the womb: I am the Lord, the Maker of all things, who stretches out the heavens, who spreads out the earth by myself."* (Isa. 44:22–24)

Other Original Testament examples can be found in *Lamentations, Hosea, Micah,* and *Zechariah*; and the New Testament furnishes seven more in *Luke, Galatians, Titus,* and *1 Peter*.

The idea of personal redemption doesn't carry much clout in twenty-first-century America, yet it hasn't been that long ago—in terms of human history—that slavery was customary all over the world. In the slavery-dependent culture that witnessed the birth in the stable, almost 20 percent of the population would have been indentured servants of one kind or another. In many, if not most, of these situations, personal debt alone was enough to force someone into servitude. Redemption was up close and personal for them.

The prolific use of the concept of redemption throughout the OT is a clear indication that the Messiah's role as our Redeemer is a critical factor in our salvation, one we need to understand.

> *Since you call on a Father who judges each person's work impartially, live out your time as foreigners here in reverent fear. For you know that it was not with perishable things such as silver or gold that you were redeemed from the empty way of life handed down to you from your ancestors, but with the precious blood of Christ, a lamb without blemish or defect. He was chosen before the creation of the world, but was revealed in these last times for your sake.* (1 Pet.1:17–20)

The major distinction between salvation and redemption is that the redeemer pays the cost that settles up the debts of the offender. Our Redeemer did not attempt to evade paying the full price for us. His love extends even to sentencing His only begotten Son to a brutal, sadistic death—Himself in human form, His Word made flesh—to satisfy the judgment we earned when we disregarded Him and chose a lie instead.

He loves us. He loves you. He paid the price to rescue us from the slave market.

The entire OT book of *Ruth* is an exposition of the guardian-redeemer concept, and it also features a marriage as the outcome. (Are you hearing this?)

The book of Ruth is set in Bethlehem, which can be translated "House of Bread." Ruth, a foreign widow, follows the advice of her Jewish mother-in-law Naomi, goes to where Boaz, a wealthy landowner, is sleeping (outdoors, possibly tipsy as a result of the harvest celebrations) and lies down at his feet. This is certainly shameless and forbidden behavior. He had already noticed her among the gleaners and shown her preferential teatment.

> *"Who are you?" he asked. "I am your servant Ruth,"* she said. *"Spread the corner of your garment over me, since you are a guardian-redeemer of our family." ".Although it is true that I am a guardian-redeemer of our family, there is another who is more closely related than I.* (It seems that he had already been considering the situation.) *Stay here for the night, and in the morning if he wants to do his duty as your guardian-redeemer, good; let him redeem you. But if he is not willing, as surely as the Lord lives I will do it. Lie here until morning."* (Ruth 3:9, 12–13)

When Naomi, wise to the ways of men, heard what had happened, she said:

> *"Wait, my daughter, until you find out what happens. For the man will not rest until the matter is settled today."* (Ruth 3:18)

And indeed, she told the truth. Naomi and Boaz married and became the great-grandparents of King David, earning official recognition in the geneology of the Messiah.

This narrative and others in the Bible demonstrate clearly that romantic love, or sexual attraction, is blessed by the Creator, part of His plan for human families. Sexual attraction is quite possibly the most powerful influence on human behavior, making it a high-value target of the adversary.

You certainly don't have to look far to find evidence of that.

CHAPTER 10

Ears to Hear
Metaphorical Consistency

We also have the prophetic message as something completely reliable… <u>no prophecy of Scripture came about by the prophet's own interpretation of things.</u> For prophecy never had its origin in the human will, but prophets, though human, spoke from God.
—2 Pet. 1:19–21

For whatever is hidden is meant to be disclosed, and whatever is concealed is meant to be brought out into the open. If anyone has ears to hear, let them hear.
—Mark 4:22–23

It is the glory of God to conceal a matter; to search out a matter is the glory of kings.
—Prov. 25:2

Let the wise listen and add to their learning, and let the discerning get guidance—for understanding proverbs and parables, the sayings and riddles of the wise. The fear of the Lord is the beginning of knowledge, but fools despise wisdom and instruction.
—Prov. 1:5–7

First things first:

Right now, you should discard, or at least hide, all the scriptural, spiritual, devotional, inspirational self-help texts that you have. Books, calendars, booklets, pamphlets, notepads, whatever you have. Pitch them. You're making space for the Word of God.

Find a translation—NOT a paraphrase—of the Bible that you are comfortable with. This is very easy in the digital age. (Check Appendix 3 for some guidance if you need it.)

Read the Bible every day. Even one chapter is okay, just do it every day, in exactly the same way you would take vitamins or brush your teeth. Don't jump around randomly. A good way to start would be to choose a book in the Hebrew Scriptures and read it one chapter at a time. *Genesis* is a remarkable narrative in any context; just pick it up and read it like you would any book. If you want something a little less challenging, *Ruth* and *Esther* each present the biographical account of a woman—one a queen the other a foreign widow—who was influential in Israel's history. The story of Jonah, short and simple to read, can be a profound revelation to those seeking to hear God.

The objective is simply to <u>get the words into your consciousness;</u> then, when the teachable moment arrives, the Holy Spirit—a manifestation of the Creator's infinite persona—will bring the relevant scripture to your mind, and you will experience the unforgettable aha moment. Then it becomes indelibly yours, inscribed on your heart.

Read the Bible for no other reason than to find out what it says. If you want to do a topic or word study, that is wonderful, but that should be separate from, and cannot replace, the chapter-a-day discipline. Stop telling God what you want to know and stop leaning on what others say about Him. Instead, find out what He wants to tell <u>you</u>. Ask Him to help you.

Ears to Hear: Metaphorical Consistency

Jesus uses the phrase "ears to hear" in Matthew chapter 13 while teaching his disciples to recognize the metaphors in God's written Word. Notice that in His explanations of figures of speech, symbols and metaphors used here—seed, the enemy, blazing furnace, light, and others—are consistent with the *Mazzaroth*. (This is why a paraphrase, rather than a translation, of the Bible is invalid.)

That same day Jesus went out of the house and sat by the lake. Such large crowds gathered around him that he got into a boat and sat in it, while all the people stood on the shore. Then he told them many things in parables, saying: "A farmer went out to sow his seed. As he was scattering the seed, some fell along the path, and the birds came and ate it up. Some fell on rocky places, where it did not have much soil. It sprang up quickly, because the soil was shallow. But when the sun came up, the plants were scorched, and they withered because they had no root. Other seed fell among thorns, which grew up and choked the plants. Still other seed fell on good soil, where it produced a crop—a hundred, sixty or thirty times what was sown. Whoever has ears, let them hear."

The disciples came to him and asked, "Why do you speak to the people in parables?" He replied, "Because the knowledge of the secrets of the kingdom of heaven has been given to you, but not to them. Whoever has will be given more, and they will have an abundance. Whoever does not have, even what they have will be taken from them. This is why I speak to them in parables: "Though seeing, they do not see; though hearing, they do not hear or understand. In them is fulfilled the prophecy of Isaiah:

"'You will be ever hearing but never understanding; you will be ever seeing but never

perceiving. For this people's heart has become calloused; they hardly hear with their ears, and they have closed their eyes. Otherwise they might see with their eyes, hear with their ears, understand with their hearts and turn, and I would heal them."

But blessed are your eyes because they see, and your ears because they hear. For truly I tell you, many prophets and righteous people longed to see what you see but did not see it, and to hear what you hear, but did not hear it.

Listen then to what the parable of the sower means: When anyone hears the message about the kingdom and does not understand it, the evil one comes and snatches away what was sown in their heart. This is the seed sown along the path. The seed falling on rocky ground refers to someone who hears the word and at once receives it with joy. But since they have no root, they last only a short time. When trouble or persecution comes because of the word, they quickly fall away. The seed falling among the thorns refers to someone who hears the word, but the worries of this life and the deceitfulness of wealth choke the word, making it unfruitful. But the seed falling on good soil refers to someone who hears the word and understands it. This is the one who produces a crop, yielding a hundred, sixty or thirty times what was sown."

...Then he left the crowd and went into the house. His disciples came to him and said, "Explain to us the parable of the weeds in the field." He answered, "The one who sowed the good seed is the Son of Man. The field is the world, and the good seed stands for the people of the kingdom. The weeds are the people of the evil one, and the enemy who sows them is the devil. The harvest is the end of the age, and the harvesters are angels. As the weeds are

pulled up and burned in the fire, so it will be at the end of the age. The Son of Man will send out his angels, and they will weed out of his kingdom everything that causes sin and all who do evil. They will throw them into the blazing furnace, where there will be weeping and gnashing of teeth. Then the righteous will shine like the sun in the kingdom of their Father. Whoever has ears, let them hear...

When Jesus had finished these parables, he moved on from there. Coming to his hometown, he began teaching the people in their synagogue, and they were amazed. "Where did this man get this wisdom and these miraculous powers?" they asked. "Isn't this the carpenter's son? Isn't his mother's name Mary, and aren't his brothers James, Joseph, Simon and Judas? Aren't all his sisters with us? Where then did this man get all these things?" And they took offense at him. But Jesus said to them, "A prophet is not without honor except in his own town and in his own home." And he did not do many miracles there because of their lack of faith. (Matt. 13)

This passage is a prophetic fulfillment of Psalm 78:1–3:

My people, hear my teaching;
listen to the words of my mouth.
I will open my mouth with a parable;
I will utter hidden things, things from of old—
things we have heard and known,
things our ancestors have told us.

Each of these parables, and the explanations that Jesus gives for them, makes it clear that <u>hearing is the responsibility of the listener.</u> The preconceptions of Jesus's childhood neighbors distorted the message in their ears, making it offensive to them. (As in the *Mazzaroth*, the river of life brings blessing to the righteous but judgment to the unrighteous.) He could do it; they could not receive it. The disability is in the receiver, not the giver. Other scriptures also mention that those with closed ears find the word of the Lord odious:

> *To whom can I speak and give warning? Who will listen to me? Their ears are closed so they cannot hear. The word of the Lord is offensive to them; they find no pleasure in it.* (Jer. 6:10)

This is another of those paradoxes of spiritual truth; what is wonderful to the believer is irritating to the unbeliever.

> *But thanks be to God, who always leads us as captives in Christ's triumphal procession and uses us to spread the aroma of the knowledge of him everywhere. For we are to God the pleasing aroma of Christ among those who are being saved and those who are perishing. To the one we are an aroma that brings death; to the other, an aroma that brings life.* (2 Cor. 2:14–16)

Twelve times the Bible admonishes the reader, "If you have ears to hear, listen" (Jer. 9:20; Mark 4:9, 23; Luke 8:8, 14:35; Rev. 2:7, 11, 17, 29; 3:6, 13, 22). Lack of hearing indicates rebellion:

> "*Son of man, you are living among a rebellious people. They have eyes to see but do not see and ears to hear but do not hear, for they are a rebellious people.*" (Ezek. 12:2)

> *For the time will come when people will not put up with sound doctrine. Instead, to suit their own desires, they will gather around them a great number of teachers to say what their itching ears want to hear.* (2 Tim. 4:3)

In contrast, the hearing believer will not lack direction from the Lord:

> *Whether you turn to the right or to the left, your ears will hear a voice behind you, saying, "This is the way; walk in it."* (Isa. 30:21)

Educators know that inspired and effective teaching is largely the result of an audience who have ears to hear. If people are listening for God, He will speak to them; the responsibility of a teacher is to maintain ears open to the Holy Spirit and to know the subject. But even so, if the assembly is primarily interested in having their preconceptions confirmed, the teaching that takes place will be disappointing for all (unless, of course, the Holy Spirit intervenes in another way).

A couple of definitions are in order here:

A symbol is something tangible used to signify something intangible, or an object used to signify a concept. Jesus explained the symbolism in the parables for the disciples; those symbols retain their specific meaning wherever they appear in the Bible (object = concept).

good seed = people of the kingdom
sower = the Son of Man
weeds = people of the evil one
enemy = the devil
harvesters = angels

If a symbol is arithmetic, a metaphor is more like algebra, signifying a relationship, like an analogy. A relates to B in the same way C relates to D. For example, the functions of a church can be correlated to the functions of a human physical body. (A:B::C:D) (A is to B as C is to D)

A personal account:

Fairly early in my serious Bible reading (early eighties), I began to use the statement, "The Bible answers its own questions." On one of the first occasions, I realized that when Jesus told His disciples they would bear good fruit and it would remain, He didn't mean lots of converts. The metaphor is defined in *Galatians*: the fruit of the Spirit is love, joy, peace, patience, kindness, goodness, gentleness, faithfulness, and self-control.

I also discovered that in the familiar armor of God passage in Ephesians chapter 6, each piece of armor is defined somewhere as the Lord Himself.

<u>Belt of truth</u>

> *Jesus answered, "I am the way and the truth and the life. No one comes to the Father except through me."* (John 14:6)

<u>Breastplate of righteousness</u>

> *It is because of him that you are in Christ Jesus, who has become for us wisdom from God—that is, our righteousness, holiness and redemption.* (1 Cor. 1:30)

<u>Feet fitted with the readiness that comes from the gospel of peace</u>

> *So Gideon built an altar to the Lord there and called it The Lord Is Peace.* (Judg. 6:24)

> *And he will be our peace.* (Mic. 5:5)

Shield of faith

> *After this, the word of the Lord came to Abram in a vision: "Do not be afraid, Abram. I am your shield, your very great reward."* (Gen. 15:1)

> *Fixing our eyes on Jesus, the pioneer and perfecter of faith.* (Heb. 12:2)

Helmet of salvation

> *The Lord is my strength and my defense; he has become my salvation.* (Exod. 15:2)

Sword of the Spirit, which is the word of God

> *In the beginning was the Word, and the Word was with God, and the Word was God.* (two for the price of one—John 1:1)

Putting on the armor of God is like climbing into a Jesus suit, the same way an astronaut climbs into a space suit. Mull that over a bit. In the world, but not of the world…

For a couple of years, I prayed that the Lord would give me the mind of Christ. To be frank, I secretly felt that having the mind of Christ would give me spiritual superiority, that I would be above the fray and universally admired. I knew the Bible answered its own questions, as noted above, but I was entirely unprepared when I came across Philippians 2:5, which begins, *"Have the same mind in you which is also in Christ Jesus."* Ah! The answer to my prayer! Then I read further:

> *In your relationships with one another, have the same mindset as Christ Jesus:* [In your relationship with your husband]

> *Who, being in very nature God, did not consider equality with God* [recognizing that you are equal to your husband] *something to be used to his own advantage*; [do not use that equality to get your own way] *rather, he made himself nothing by taking the very nature of a servant,* [but become his servant, making his goals your goals] *being made in human likeness* [matching your endeavors to his endeavors] *And being found in appearance as a man, he humbled himself* [consider your pursuits less important than his] *by becoming obedient to death—even death on a stake!* [even giving up your own identity] *Therefore God exalted him to the highest place and gave him the name that is above every name, that at the name of Jesus every knee should bow, in heaven and on earth and under the earth, and every tongue acknowledge that Jesus Christ is Lord, to the glory of God the Father.* (Phil. 2:5–11)

This was not exactly what I was expecting. Another spiritual paradox: the way up is down. The way to win is to surrender. Eternal life is the result of death to self. Spiritual authority cannot increase without self-sacrifice. My true God-purposed identity can blossom only when I kill the false identity I've been using all my life.

About this time, my assertion had evolved into "The Bible defines itself," and I was beginning to ponder the concept of metaphorical consistency.

I was finding that throughout both testaments of the Bible, every symbol and every metaphor is always specifically defined somewhere in one of the texts and retains its meaning throughout the whole book. Regardless of intervening centuries and diverse writers, if a fig tree symbolizes human judgment in *Genesis* (Adam and Eve made aprons of fig leaves to cover their nakedness), it will be used the same way in *Matthew*. If thorns signify human toil in *Genesis* (the earth would bring forth thorns for Adam, and he would get food by the sweat of his brow) it will be the same throughout the entire narrative.

Jesus cursed a fruitless fig tree when he entered Jerusalem before appearing to the Sanhedrin, the Jewish governing body, and He died crowned with Adam's thorns.

> *We also have the prophetic message as something <u>completely reliable</u>, and you will do well to pay attention to it, as to a light shining in a dark place, until the day dawns and the morning star rises in your hearts. Above all, you must understand that* **no prophecy of Scripture came about by the prophet's own interpretation of things.** *For prophecy never had its origin in the human will, but prophets, though human, spoke from God as they were carried along by the Holy Spirit.* (2 Pet. 1:19–21)

As Peter states, no prophet personally created the metaphors that appear in his prophecies, because **all biblical metaphors, wherever they appear, are specifically defined somewhere in the text. The Bible's message is absolutely reliable.**

> *It is the glory of God to conceal a matter; it is the glory of kings to search it out.* (Prov. 25:2)

Revelation 19:8 states that fine linen is the righteousness of saints. This means that we can go back to the beginning of *Genesis*, knowing that any mention of fine linen anywhere in the Bible will give an insight into righteousness (linen = righteousness). No one can assign another symbolic meaning to linen; the Bible provides the specific definition. Similarly, Revelation 5:8 states that the incense at God's throne signifies the prayers of the saints (incense = prayer). Also, the Word of God is living and active, like a double-edged sword (Word = sword).

I can picture Paul and Apollos, bent over a scroll in candlelight, overwhelmed with revelation and then going out and proving from the Scriptures that Jesus of Nazareth is inarguably the promised Messiah.

The Bible's metaphorical consistency cannot be coincidental or the product of human collaboration. It is conclusive evidence, proving that in spite of many writers over many generations, God is the only author of the Bible. It is His Word.

Except there were a couple of problems. When the Israelites were beset with poisonous snakes while wandering through the wilderness, why did Moses hang the brazen serpent, obviously a prophetic reference to the Savior, on a pole? That didn't correlate to any of the NT accounts of His death on a cross. And there's another Messianic verse that refers to a "peg hung in a sure place." And for metaphorical consistency to be valid, it has to be 100 percent accurate.

That bothered me. A lot. And then...

I received a book in the mail from a lifelong friend, with a note saying she thought I might need it. It was *The Aramaic-English NT*, by Andrew Gabriel Roth. I learned from that book—along with a measureless treasure trove of New Testament information—that the word *cross* never appears anywhere in the Bible. Never. Nowhere. Original Testament or New Testament. Jesus was hung on a wooden pole or "execution stake."

Knock me down with a feather.

The discrepancy, apparently, can be safely attributed to St. Jerome, who translated the Greek Septuagint into the Latin Vulgate and whose primary objective was to eliminate all traces of Judaism from Christianity. (More about this elsewhere.)

Does it really matter that much? Well, for one thing, picking up your staff, a symbol of authority, to follow Jesus, is something quite different from picking up your cross to follow Him. But more troublesome material appeared.

> On the contrary: "If your enemy is hungry, feed him; if he is thirsty, give him something to drink. In

doing this, you will heap burning coals on his head." (Rom. 12:20)

This verse came across, nearly simultaneously, a couple of the websites I looked at, and in both places, it was stated that the "burning coals on his head" actually refered to lifesaving coals being transported in a container on top of someone's head. That is certainly a reasonable conclusion, except that burning coals are not mentioned in a positive way anywhere else in the Bible. The closest to it is the use of burning coals to present incense in the temple.

Otherwise:

Smoke rose from his nostrils; consuming fire came from his mouth, burning coals blazed out of it. (2 Sam. 22:9)

On the wicked he will rain fiery coals and burning sulfur; a scorching wind will be their lot. (Ps. 11:6)

He will punish you with a warrior's sharp arrows, with burning coals of the broom bush. (Ps. 120:4)

May burning coals fall on them; may they be thrown into the fire, into miry pits, never to rise. (Ps. 140:10)

In doing this, you will heap burning coals on his head, and the Lord will reward you. (Prov. 25:22)

Another tricky issue is the word *leaven*, which is almost always identified as a symbol for sin. Cleaning the house of leaven is, of course, a major component of observing Passover. Jesus told his disciples to avoid the leaven of the Pharisees, but He also compared it to the kingdom of God:

> *Again he asked, "What shall I compare the kingdom of God to? It is like yeast that a woman took and mixed into about sixty pounds of flour until it worked all through the dough."* (Luke 13:20–21)

Obviously this is a positive, not a negative, reference. Looking a little further, though, we find this passage:

> *Your boasting is not good. Don't you know that a little yeast leavens the whole batch of dough? Get rid of the old yeast, so that you may be a new unleavened batch—as you really are. For Christ, our Passover lamb, has been sacrificed. Therefore let us keep the Festival, not with the old bread leavened with malice and wickedness, but with the unleavened bread of sincerity and truth.* (1 Cor. 5:6–8)

The metaphor (Christ = Passover lamb) happens to be defined here, but that's not what we're focusing on right now, although you can bet it's a significant detail. This is getting confusing. Let's go back to the leaven of the Pharisees. And READ THE WHOLE PASSAGE.

> *"Be careful," Jesus said to them. "Be on your guard against the yeast of the Pharisees and Sadducees." They discussed this among themselves and said, "It is because we didn't bring any bread." Aware of their discussion, Jesus asked, "You of little faith, why are you talking among yourselves about having no bread? Do you still not understand? Don't you remember the five loaves for the five thousand, and how many basketfuls you gathered? Or the seven loaves for the four thousand, and how many basketfuls you gathered? How is it you don't understand that I was not talking to you about bread? But be on your guard against the yeast of the Pharisees and Sadducees." <u>Then they understood that he was not telling them</u>*

> <u>*to guard against the yeast used in* **bread**, *but against the* **teaching** *of the* Pharisees and Sadducees.</u> (Matt. 16:6–12)

Well. That's a specific definition, for sure. A woman's teaching can nourish a whole town, apparently. Religious leaders, not so much. But what about the unleavened bread and cleansing the house from leaven? If leaven means teaching, then unleavened must mean untaught.

Oh my.

A Sunday school teacher I admired used to say about the gospel: "It's not a learned truth; it's a revealed truth." Look at the verses that immediately follow the above passage in Matthew 16:

> *When Jesus came to the region of Caesarea Philippi, he asked his disciples, "Who do people say the Son of Man is?" They replied, "Some say John the Baptist; others say Elijah; and still others, Jeremiah or one of the prophets." "But what about you?" he asked. "Who do you say I am?" Simon Peter answered, "You are the Messiah, the Son of the living God." Jesus replied, "Blessed are you, Simon son of Jonah, for this was not revealed to you by flesh and blood, but by my Father in heaven.* (Matt. 16:13–17)

1 Corinthians 5:6–8 becomes a revelation.

The gospel, eternal life, cannot be learned or earned; it is the free gift of God.

<u>Metaphorical consistency indicates clearly that the Bible is not the product of human effort or ingenuity.</u>

Additionally, every aspect of nature also serves as a metaphor that God uses to reveal Himself to us. *Psalm* 22 is widely recognized to be a prophetic vision of the suffering and death of our Redeemer, even though it was written one thousand years before the execution of Jesus. But verses 6–8 contain a startling image:

> *But I am a worm and not a man, scorned by everyone, despised by the people. All who see me mock me; they hurl insults, shaking their heads. "He trusts in the Lord," they say, "let the Lord rescue him. Let him deliver him, since he delights in him."* (Ps. 22:6–8)

The verse says, *"But I am a worm and not a man."* Jesus was certainly a man, so what did the psalmist mean when he wrote, *"But I am a worm"*? Two words are translated "worm" in the Original Testament; one of them means a maggot. The other is a grub-like worm, sometimes called the crimson worm, common in the Middle East, valuable for its use in making red dye. This is the one David is speaking of in Psalm 22.

When the female crimson worm is ready to lay her eggs, she attaches herself to a wooden tree or fence (a stake). A hard crimson shell forms around her and attaches her securely to the wood so that it would kill her to try to scrape it off. She lays her eggs under her body, and when the larvae hatch underneath the shell, they commence feeding on the still-living mother worm for three days. When she dies, her body excretes a vivid red liquid that permanently stains both the wood and the baby worms. The fourth day, the mother worm retracts into her head, forming a heart-shaped body that becomes a white wax, looking like a patch of wool on the wood. It then begins to flake off and drop to the ground looking like snow. Are you hearing this?

> *Come now, and let us reason together, saith the* Lord: *though your sins be as scarlet, they shall be as white as snow: though they be red like crimson, they shall be as wool.* (Isa 1:18)

> *Ears that hear and eyes that see—the Lord has made them both.* (Prov. 20:12)

The crimson worm's body and shell, while still red and attached to the tree, are scraped off and used to make what is called royal red dye. In biblical times, the red dye excreted from the crimson worm (Ps 22:6, Isa 1:18, Isa. 66:24) provided the color used in the high priest's robe. The waxy material is shellac that is used in the Middle East as a wood preservative. The remains of the crimson worm are also used in pharmaceutical treatment for heart problems. It's also interesting to note that the cardinal (avian) was so named because the cardinals of the Catholic Church wear this color, not vice versa.

The crimson worm is only one example of the Creator revealing Himself through his creation. There are many, many more. In fact, every natural phenomenon, every single one, reveals Him to those with ears to hear. "He became poor." Jesus became a worm. He was crushed for our sakes, and we receive life from His blood that washes us clean. Look at Psalm 22; Jesus quoted this psalm during His execution, when He cried:

"My God, my God, why hast thou forsaken me?"
(Matt. 27:46, Mark 15:34).

The Creator established physical laws that govern the material world, from the tiniest particle to largest galaxy. These laws also serve as metaphors that reveal Him to us. Gravity is the ultimate constant—we know when, where, and how much, but no one knows exactly why.

He holds the worlds together by the word of His power. (Heb. 1:3, Col. 1:17)

All organic things, plants and animals, their life cycles and communities, serve as living metaphors, revealing God's nature to those who have ears to hear. They declare God's word to us in a language we can understand, if we choose to hear it.

Possibly the most courageous act any of us are ever called to do is make the decision to follow Jesus; to be a doer, not just a hearer. As one enlightened soul expressed it: God doesn't want your commitment; He wants your surrender. Ironically (or paradoxically), this act of surrender is completely internal—undetectable with any of our five senses. But our deceptive nature, soul, inner man, psyche, persona, schema, inscape, and others is not going down without a fight. It is determined to retain control, and in this case, <u>a triumph of the human spirit is not a good thing.</u>

Every single good thing about us—talents, abilities, and other more intangible attributes—is given to us by our Creator. We don't even know what our true capabilities are until we allow our Father to educate us. The same thing is true about our negative traits. The only thing of our own that we can offer Him is our decision to believe and be honest. Let's review:

Nobody should be dependent on someone else's Bible reading.
God created man because He wanted to be a father.
God never rejects anybody.
Sin ignites God's wrath, and His wrath cannot be restrained.
You don't get to decide what God is like.
Truth is the only language you can speak to God.
You must set your will to obey Him first of all.
The only thing God requires from you is honesty.
The result of honesty is always humility.
Eternal life can not be learned or earned.
Satan's only weapon is to make you believe something that is not true.

When you hear and obey, unimagined wonders become part of your normal routine.

CHAPTER 11
Forsaken Stars

And God said, 'Let there be lights in the vault of the sky to separate the day from the night, and let them serve as signs to mark sacred times, and days and years, and let them be lights in the vault of the sky to give light on the earth.' And it was so.
—Gen. 1:14–15

He determines the number of the stars and calls them each by name.
—Psalm 147:4

From the beginning, God intended the visible stars and planets (called wandering stars by the ancients) for man's use, to keep track of time and as signals for holy events, in addition to providing visible light. Furthermore, the metaphorical use of the term *light* as an indicator of God's word is consistent throughout the Bible; metaphorically, the stars giving light also means they are a source of revelation about God, as well as physical lights in the sky. Even the most distressed souls can receive a kind of peace when looking at the stars, although they don't know why. God is always blessing and revealing Himself to mankind through every available channel.

> *For all the gods of the nations are idols, but the Lord made the heavens.* (1 Chron. 16:26)

> *For the Lord is great and greatly to be praised: He is to be feared above all gods. For all the gods of the nations are idols, but the Lord made the heavens.* (Ps. 96:4–5)

The sky has been continually scrutinized and its every characteristic recorded since the beginning of human history. The visibility of the night sky has been greatly impaired in modern times because of ambient light from the earth combined with pollution. Early humans had a much sharper view and nothing much to pass the time after dark except study the sky.

Ancient cultures all over the globe have demonstrated a sophisticated understanding of the behavior of celestial bodies. Knowledge of the forty-eight constellations seen with the naked eye, beginning with Virgo and ending with Leo, also seem to have been universal common knowledge from the earliest recorded times.

Newton believed that the Creator was a God of logic and order, a concept well established in the Bible, and his definition of the three laws of motion made it possible, for the first time, to calculate the movements of objects in space. Newton's first law, the law of inertia, states that a body at rest tends to stay at rest, and a body in motion tends to stay in motion, unless acted on by an external force. His second law expresses the relationship between force, velocity, and mass; a force causes a change in velocity (how much depends on mass), or a change in velocity produces force. The third law states that for every action in nature, there is an equal and opposite reaction. Using these three laws, the location of any heavenly object can be pinpointed, and future movement and positions can be calculated.

Newton's laws support the "God as clockmaker" concept; once the universe was in motion, every subsequent event was predestined, that is, determined by the behavior of particles in motion. Furthermore, the clock can be "turned back" as well, to identify past positions; that's how the big bang theory was formulated. The phenomenon of the Bethlehem star, which signaled the birth of the promised Messiah to astronomers in the East, has been identified and confirmed in this way.

On the other hand, the discovery of quantum mechanics revealed that not all objects obey Newton's laws. The fact that some subatomic particles achieve reality only as a result of being observed, while the behavior of the object they inhabit continues to conform to Newton's laws is nothing if not paradoxical. Spiritual laws, as equally binding as physical laws, are paradoxical in the same way; for example, the long-standing debate about free will versus predestination is not either/or, but both/and, just as light is both a particle (predestination) and a wave (free will/choice).

Note:

Evidently, some particles exist only while being observed. That's an intriguing concept, isn't it? Think about it this way:

You're in a room where a group of people are holding a meeting. How many words are in that room? The number of words contained in each person's vocabulary, added to the words of the others (excluding repetitions) is an incomprehensible but finite amount. However, only the words selected for use become "real." Those are the words that are spoken by someone, are transcribed into the meeting minutes, and heard on the audio recording. The real words—the creative ones—are the ones that are used.

Every human being ever conceived—requiring male sperm and female egg—is made in the image of God, and our Father destined mankind from the beginning to be eternally in communion with Him. Each of us is predestined to become one with Him; that's why He created us. However, our determined efforts to create and maintain an identity outside of His presence, hiding from Him, avoiding the light, makes it impossible for us to fulfill that destiny. Yet He continues to reveal Himself to us in whatever manner we can receive, constantly calling us home. The beauty of the stars is an example of how He is continually attracting us into His presence.

> *It is the glory of God to conceal a matter; it is the glory of kings to search it out.* (Prov. 25:2)

God reveals His mysteries in the created universe; the universe is intended to be a material exhibition of His character and attributes. As humans investigate and study our environment, we continue to gain more understanding about natural processes that are confirmed by His Word.

For example, many Bible verses refer to God "stretching out the heavens" (Isa. 40:22, Isa. 42:5, Isa. 44:24, Isa. 45:12, Isa. 48:13, Isa. 51:13, Jer. 10:12, Job 9:8, Ps.104:2), an intriguing figure of speech. Picture a deflated balloon that has constellations drawn on it by making dots with a permanent marker. Now, picture that balloon being inflated. The heavens are being "stretched out" as air fills the balloon, a precise illustration of the (fairly) recently postulated "expanding universe"—all those particles suddenly exploding outward from the big bang. Another peculiarly apt metaphor used in the Word of God before the technology existed to describe the actual event!

> *Dominion and awe belong to God; he establishes order in the heights of heaven.* (Job 25:2)

Both *Psalm* 136 and *Proverbs* 3 state that God made the heavens by understanding.

Another consistent biblical motif is that God Himself named and placed each star.

> *It is I who made the earth and created mankind on it. My own hands stretched out the heavens; I marshaled their starry hosts.* (Isa. 45:12)

> *"To whom will you compare me? Or who is my equal?" says the Holy One. Lift up your eyes and look to the heavens: Who created all these? He who brings out the starry host one by one and calls forth each of them by name. Because of his great power and mighty strength, not one of them is missing.* (Isa. 40:25–26)

David as a shepherd spent many nights alone under the stars, considering their behavior and pondering their message. He was a poet and a prophet, as well as a warrior, known as a man "after God's own heart." He wrote:

> *By the word of the Lord the heavens were made, their starry host by the breath of his mouth.* (Ps. 33:6)

and

> *He determines the number of the stars and calls them each by name.* (Ps. 147:4)

and

> *Lord, our Lord, how majestic is your name in all the earth! You have set your glory in the heavens. Through the praise of children and infants you have established a stronghold against your enemies, to silence the foe and the avenger. When I consider your heavens, the work of your fingers, the moon and the stars, which you have set in place, what is mankind that you are mindful of them, human beings that you care for them?* (Ps. 8:1–4)

> *The heavens proclaim his righteousness, for he is a God of justice.* (Ps. 50:6)

> *The heavens praise your wonders, Lord, your faithfulness too, in the assembly of the holy ones.* (Ps. 89:5)

> *The heavens proclaim his righteousness, and all peoples see his glory.* (Ps. 97:6)

Psalm 19 is an especially fascinating example of David's knowledge of the heavens and their message from the Creator. This psalm attests that God has made a special habitation for the sun, notes the circuit through the heavens that the sun travels from day to day, and states that nothing is outside its warmth. Today, science has confirmed this astounding fact, that like every object in the universe, our sun maintains a particular orbit through its galaxy and across the universe and is exerting its force on every other object.

> *The heavens declare the glory of God; the skies proclaim the work of his hands. Day after day they pour forth speech; night after night they reveal knowledge. They have no speech, they use no words; no sound is heard from them. Yet their voice goes out into all the earth, their words to the ends of the world. In the heavens God has pitched a tent for the sun. It is like a bridegroom coming out of his chamber, like a champion rejoicing to run his course. It rises at one end of the heavens and makes its circuit to the other; nothing is deprived of its warmth.* (Ps. 19:1–6)

The truth that God is the Creator was the basis of the Apostle Paul's declaration of the gospel to his audiences everywhere. In Acts 17, Paul stood to speak in the open forum of the Areopagus, where Greek philosophers and students came to expound and debate current issues. After surveying the Acropolis, Paul began his appeal:

> *"People of Athens! I see that in every way you are very religious. For as I walked around and looked carefully at your objects of worship, I even found an altar with this inscription: to an unknown god. So you are ignorant of the very thing you worship—and this is what I am going to proclaim to you.*
>
> *The God who made the world and everything in it is the Lord of heaven and earth and does not live in temples built by human hands. And he is not served by human hands, as if he needed anything. Rather, he himself gives everyone life and breath and everything else. From one man he made all the nations, that they should inhabit the whole earth; and he marked out their appointed times in history and the boundaries of their lands. God did this so that they would seek him and perhaps reach out for him and find him, though he is not far from any one of us. 'For in him we live and move and have our being.' As some of your own poets have said, 'We are his offspring.'"* (Acts 17:22–28)

In the last line of this excerpt, Paul quotes from an influential ancient work called *Phaenomena*, written in 277 BC by the Greek philosopher and astronomer Aratus. Keep in mind that, in that era, years were not numbered and, aside from the Hebrew calendar, no standardized identification of months and days existed. However, everyone everywhere was familiar with the night sky, which served as a universally recognized calendar and map.

Phaenomena, a poetic work describing the constellations, is important because it uses the original names of "the signs of the *Zodiac*" (Hebrew *Mazzaroth*), which are Hebrew and Arabic in origin. These names were common knowledge before Claudius Ptolemy (the father of modern astrology) produced the *Almagest*, some three centuries later, in which he modified the constellation names to correlate with Greek and Roman mythology. Claudius

Ptolemy also invented horoscopic astrology, and his *Almagest* is the source cited by astrologers today.

The same version of the zodiac found in *Phaenomena*, the original, was discovered inside the Denderah Sphinx during Napolean's Egyptian campaign in about AD 1800. It was marked with complex lines, arcs, and symbols that indicate sophisticated mathematical understanding of star movements. The dating of the Denderah zodiac is controversial, with wildly differing estimates, but all agree that this planisphere (map of the sky, or star map) commonly cited as an illustration of Egyptian astrological beliefs, predates the Greco-Roman version.

The Denderah planisphere is a discovery that disappointed scientists; VictorianWeb Science states that "its existence posed no problems for Mosaic chronology. Scientists were not overjoyed to hear this news. The Pope, however, was so grateful to Champollion for saving traditional biblical chronology that he offered to make the Republican, nonreligious, and very married Champollion a cardinal."

If God did place the stars and name them, and if they are meant to communicate His word to us, as the Bible indicates, how can we learn what that message is?

> "Can you bind the chains of the Pleiades? Can you loosen Orion's belt? Can you bring forth the constellations in their seasons or lead out the Bear with its cubs?" (Job 38:31–32)

The book of *Job* is a very ancient text, conservatively dated to 4400 BC, and yet recorded here are familiar names of constellations. If Job already knew the names of the constellations, then who named them?

A book called *Mazzaroth*—the Hebrew word for constellations—is the life's work of a woman named Frances Rolleston. In *Mazzaroth*, Rolleston identified the etymological root for each original star and constellation name, all of which are Hebrew or Arabic in origin, then traced the use of those root words through the Hebrew scriptures, thereby revealing their forgotten message. She can in no way be called an astrologist; her work (completed in the 1860s) cannot be applied to personal horoscopes or fortune-telling, which is what blasphemous astrology deals with.

Modern horoscope astrologers believe that the signs of the zodiac are an ancient but random selection of stars, as the constellations do indeed appear to be. No one sees an actual goat shape in the stars, but a collection of stars that have been named Capricorn, which, like the other signs, has always been pictured the same bizarre way in zodiac drawings: a goat facing to the left with its head down, front legs splayed, and a twisting fish tail instead of a rump; sometimes it is called a sea-goat. Any one of us could go out on a clear night and make up our own pictures that would be just as accurate. Why were these particular star clusters—forty-eight constellations, the twelve major signs, each with its own set of three decans—so early settled that every culture recognized them? (The Chinese zodiac of twelve animals is credited to Buddha, about 563 BC, earlier than *Phaenomena* but much later than *Job*.)

Note:

Recent depictions of the zodiac sometimes include drawings that do not exactly match the originals. For example, Capricorn, the sea-goat, might not have the correctly splayed legs in front, or Virgo, the virgin, might be shown with wings, as if she were an angel. These modern planispheres seem to indicate that current devotees of astrology are ignorant of the ancient, but eternally relevant, messages that are conveyed by the images.

Set aside your disbelief for a moment and consider the situation. Adam, a real human being, had committed a grievous blunder that he could not undo, and he knew that he had brought a devastating curse on humanity and the earth; he had heard God pronounce it with his own ears: from dust you came, to dust you will return. Eve and the serpent had also been cursed, but God had not left people without hope. God Himself pronounced the first prophecy of the coming Messiah, who would be born of woman and suffer injury, but who would crush the enemy of God and man:

> *I will put enmity between you and the woman, and between your offspring and hers; he will crush your head, and you will strike his heel.* (Gen. 3:15)

Adam fully realized that this promise revealed humanity's only hope for achieving the eternal life God had predestined for mankind. He knew that grasping and retaining this promise from God was of vital significance for coming generations. Ignorance would result in the most severe consequences imaginable—eternal separation from God, meaninglessness, and death. Adam knew the promise and God's true purpose for mankind must be preserved in such a way that no person on earth would ever be able to miss it. God gave him the means to accomplish this.

The stars have tremendous power to inspire awe and reverence, even apart from the pictorial message of the Messiah. In order to avoid God's light, men had to devise a means to distort the way His voice is heard in nature, particularly in the sky. The devil is not called The Subtle for nothing; he understands man's arrogant self-interest and desperate need for peer approval.

Not long after the Noahic Flood, a ziggurat was built in Babel, evidence of a long-term strategy to usurp God's message for humanity: the corruption of the gospel in the sky. The confusion of the languages at Babel disrupted the collaboration needed to complete that project, but the strategy of distorting the *Mazzaroth*'s prophetic message of the Messiah remained.

<u>The perversion of the *Mazzaroth* into a means of fortune telling, witchcraft, and divination is blasphemy.</u> God called Abram to take his family and leave Ur of the Chaldeans, an urban center of star worship, and He promised Abram that he would become a great nation and a blessing to all people on earth, always carrying God's blessing wherever he went. God told Abram on more than one occasion to "consider the stars." Abram believed God and set out seeking a city whose builder and maker is God (Heb. 11:10).

Abram, renamed by God Abraham, became the father of the Jewish and Arab nations, who from infancy was told of God's promise written in the sky. Abraham first sent Ishmael, whose mother was

Egyptian, into the East, then later his other children from the wife he married after the death of Sarah. Isaac, the child of the promise, would beget Jacob (Israel), the father of the twelve tribes, including Judah, from whom the promised Lion would come. All of Abraham's descendents knew the story in the sky and were watching for the Messiah; indeed, the three Magi from the East were among the first to know.

Convincing people that celestial bodies have power and are worthy of worship is not difficult. The belief that everything in the heavens exists to enlighten me, about my own purpose, is only a small step further. The deceiver proclaims, "The stars and their movement through the sky are magnificent, mystical, and supernatural, and they are about *you* and what is special about *you* and what is going to happen to *you*. Discover your purpose in life here!" The ploy has been so effective, in fact, that in Christian zeal to avoid witchcraft and divination, the original message has been shunned as well, effectively throwing the baby out with the bathwater.

Star Speak

According to ancient Hebrew tradition, Adam, Seth, and Enoch were responsible for mapping out the heavens, thereby creating the first planisphere; certainly no one else has taken credit. Each of them lived several hundreds of overlapping years and were thus able to observe the yearly rotation of the stars many, many times. They first segmented the overhead vault into twelve equal wedge-shaped sections and then began the process of identifying each section by its most recognizable stars.

The Bible tells us that God named the stars, so those names would have been available for the men to use. The names of the stars in each section ("house") supplied them with details of the spiritual conflict precipitated by Satan's rebellion and how it would progress through history.

Consider the predicament of translating a written story from English into a language that uses an alphabet of only six letters. C. S. Lewis delivered an address during World War II entitled

"Transposition" that explicated this problem (see Appendix 2). In order to accomplish the translation, some letters would have to serve double duty, new letter combinations could be created to fill certain requirements, or new words could be invented using the available six letters.

The same problem occurs when God seeks to communicate with His human children. Some spiritual truths cannot be adequately expressed using human language or examples from nature. The story in the sky is like that; mythological beasts and metaphorical images have been designed for the purpose of depicting spiritual concepts in ways that humans can comprehend and remember. God always confirms His word, and so the written Word that we now have, the Bible, should confirm the message in the stars, if the *Mazzaroth* is indeed God's Word in the sky.

The Bible is always the standard, the final word.

The Denderah *Mazzaroth* planisphere, found inside the sphinx, indicates that the circuit begins with the constellation called Virgo (which, interestingly, concurs with Hebrew Yom Kippur) and ends with Leo. By considering the pictorial images that represent each sign and by identifying the original names of the constellations and primary stars, the message becomes unmistakable.

Psalm 89:37 states:

> *It will be established forever like the moon, the faithful witness in the sky.*

The *Mazzoroth* cycle can be divided into three sections, or chapters; each of these chapters includes four houses; each house contains a thesis (the major constellation) and three points of discussion (the decans).

The first chapter includes Virgo, Libra, Scorpio, and Sagitarrius, with their decans, and focuses on "The Christ," so that is what I have called that section.

The second chapter, consisting of Capricorn, Aquarius, Pisces, and Aries—sometimes known as the water signs—foretells the miraculous body of Christ, and I have called that section "The Church."

The third chapter, labelled here "The Consummation," deals with the end of the age and includes Taurus, Gemini, Cancer, and Leo. From Virgo, the virgin, to Leo, the lion.

You can find many planispheres online that depict the constellations in various ways. When searching, make sure you specify the Mazzaroth, not the zodiac, version.

Good News in the Heavens, Condensed

Throughout the yearly cycle of the *Mazzaroth*, star names and constellation images consistently and repetitively emphasize the gospel of the coming Messiah, who defeats the deceiver of mankind and restores humanity to our rightful position as the beloved intimate companion of God. The written Word of God in the Bible is the standard by which all other sources are measured, so the truth of the *Mazzaroth* is judged by its adherence to the Bible, not vice versa.

A Savior, a God/man born of a virgin, the hope of all people, is despised, wounded, and pierced, but utterly defeats the enemy (identified as the devil, the serpent, the dragon, or Satan) who seeks to supplant the authority of God and who leads the whole world astray.

The coming ruler is the Redeemer; He willingly pays the price to buy back the souls who have believed the lie and are in the bondage of sin. The mighty hero conquers death and hell.

He is known as the Branch, because He is born from the root of a particular people, the Hebrew nation, the children of Abraham, the tribe of Judah, the family of Jesse.

The voluntary self-sacrifice of this ruler brings into the world a new kind of people, who depend on the river of life, the outpoured Holy Spirit, for sustenance. They remain in the world but are no longer of the world. The people of God include two nations, Hebrews and Gentiles, who collectively become the physical body on earth of the Savior, awaiting His swift return.

Known as the church, this mystical entity is depicted as a chained woman awaiting deliverance. The bondage is broken by the

Lamb, slain from the foundation of the world; He is the King at the apex of creation, around whom the sky rotates.

At the end of the age, the Redeemer, a gentle shepherd to His people, will come in wrath to bring eternal judgment on the accuser and adversary of God, the serpent who defrauded mankind of our destiny.

The increasing multitudes of the redeemed, including those once considered unclean, inhabit a safe place of rest. The church in bondage is released and enthroned as a bride, an equal sovereign walking side by side with the king.

The church—consistently depicted as female—and the Savior—consistently depicted as male—become one in eternal communion and authority over creation. The same River of Life that brings healing to the church brings fiery judgment on the serpent.

* * * * *

The archetypal literature of the Bible takes on new depth of meaning when read with the understanding that the *Mazzaroth* was common knowledge to ancient peoples. The sky was their calendar, their map, their textbook, and their diversion. Noah, Hebrew patriarchs and prophets, and King David record many instances (far too many to include here) of hearing God speak or receiving revelation from Him while considering the stars. The Psalms especially, already intense, become even more profound.

The exiled Hebrews Joseph, Daniel, Ezekiel, Ezra, and Nehemiah became esteemed in pagan cultures when heathen rulers recognized that they worshiped *the God who made the heavens*. They already knew about the *Mazzaroth*; it was common knowledge, and everyone used it as a calendar and a map, and they knew the story it told. In the same way that the enemy has targeted heterosexual monogamy in his attempt to thwart the Word of God, he also has endeavored to subvert the gospel in the sky, turning it to his own purposes and depriving humanity of its real power.

The devil cannot create anything; he can only counterfeit.

CHAPTER 12

Conclusion
Satan's Haymaker and the Real Conspiracy

The centuries immediately following the execution, resurrection, and ascension of the one born in the stable were a season of intense spiritual warfare. Satan had not been successful in his attempts to kill the Messiah, and Jesus's resurrection after He was executed sealed the verdict. Satan, the dragon, the devil, the serpent, our adversary, is destined for the eternal lake of fire, which is already prepared for him. The Bible says that he is furious because he knows his time is short.

He still hates God, and he hates us. He is a powerful, cunning liar, bent on hurting as many people as possible before his time is up. He has legions of followers who do what he tells them to do. He is bent on ruining God's works, which can only be accomplished by deceiving people.

The devil's overall strategy might be summarized by these tactics:

- Corrupt the institution of marriage (undermine husband/wife relationship, discredit heterosexual monogamy)
- Sabotage the Bible (Hurray to St. Jerome)
- Counterfeit the *Mazzaroth* (Hurray, Claudius Ptolemy)
- Sever Christianity from Judaism (Hurray, Marcion)
- Substitute a bureaucratic hierarchy for the body of Christ (Hurray, to Laodicea and Nicaea)
- Convince people that a bureaucratic hierarchy is the body of Christ

The Torah is a great deal more than list of rules, and Mount Sinai was not simply a place where Moses received the law but where a *marriage covenant* was sealed between God and His people.

> *For your Maker is your husband—the Lord Almighty is his name—the Holy One of Israel is your Redeemer; he is called the God of all the earth.* (Isa. 54:5)

God's institution of marriage and heterosexual monogamy has always been Satan's highest priority target. At the beginning of history, he launched his first missile at the woman: a lie. He has nothing but lies to launch. He is a one-trick pony, but he is extremely devious with the trick he has. You remember that old adage, that the guilty always accuses his opponent of committing his own offense? Slap him with it before he has a chance to slap you, just enough to muddy the waters a little bit? The devil informed Eve that God had told her a lie about the fruit, and he said if they did eat it, they would be like gods, knowing good from evil.

Adam's mistake was allowing his wife's voice to supersede the Creator's, and he blamed her. A wedge was driven into the marriage relationship. From then on, men have been endowed with a deeply rooted suspicion of women, resulting in a profound deficiency of understanding and communication. On the other hand, women to this day carry guilt that they desperately try to assuage by allowing themselves to be victimized by oppressive male partners. Satan's first tactic was successful, and thus commenced the war between the sexes.

The war between the sexes devolved into the war on the sexes, and some might even say it has now become the war on sex itself. Our own sinful desires give Satan the means to implement his deception, which is so sad, and truly paradoxical, since it is the sin of lust that fuels the war on sex. A sort of devilish bait-and-switch, of which there are many. Disarming the enemy is accomplished merely by confessing the sin, and our Lord takes care of the rest, forgiving us and cleansing us from unrighteousness. (What does the Lord require from us? Honesty. That's all. So simple. But not easy.)

Here's a story for you. It's true.

During the New Testament era, Ephesus, in what is now Turkey, was very important to pagan worship. The temple of Artemis (Diana in Latin), which housed the famous statue that was supposed to have fallen from heaven, was located there. Artemis was the virgin goddess of the hunt. She was known as "Artemis of the Ephesians," in much the same way that a town today might be identified by its dominating sports team, like Atlanta, home of the Braves.

Ephesus attracted a lot of tourists because of the temple, and a group of artisans and silversmiths had established a thriving business selling silver statues of the goddess as mementos.

The Apostle Paul came to the town on one of his missionary journeys through the area, explaining the coming of the Messiah. Some people had begun calling the new movement "The Way." Now we'll go to Acts chapter 19:23–41:

> *About that time there arose a great disturbance about the Way. A silversmith named Demetrius, who made silver shrines of Artemis, brought in a lot of business for the craftsmen there. He called them together, along with the workers in related trades, and said: "You know, my friends, that we receive a good income from this business. And you see and hear how this fellow Paul has convinced and led*

astray large numbers of people here in Ephesus and in practically the whole province of Asia. He says that gods made by human hands are no gods at all. There is danger not only that our trade will lose its good name, but also that the temple of the great goddess Artemis will be discredited; and the goddess herself, who is worshiped throughout the province of Asia and the world, will be robbed of her divine majesty."

When they heard this, they were furious and began shouting: "Great is Artemis of the Ephesians!" Soon the whole city was in an uproar. The people seized Gaius and Aristarchus, Paul's traveling companions from Macedonia, and all of them rushed into the theater together. Paul wanted to appear before the crowd, but the disciples would not let him.

Even some of the officials of the province, friends of Paul, sent him a message begging him not to venture into the theater.

The assembly was in confusion: some were shouting one thing, some another. Most of the people did not even know why they were there. The Jews in the crowd pushed Alexander to the front, and they shouted instructions to him. He motioned for silence in order to make a defense before the people. But when they realized he was a Jew, they all shouted in unison for about two hours: "Great is Artemis of the Ephesians!"

The city clerk quieted the crowd and said: "Fellow Ephesians, doesn't all the world know that the city of Ephesus is the guardian of the temple of the great Artemis and of her image, which fell from heaven? Therefore, since these facts are undeniable, you ought to calm down and not do anything rash. You have brought these men here, though they have

Conclusion: Satan's Haymaker and the Real Conspiracy

neither robbed temples nor blasphemed our goddess. If, then, Demetrius and his fellow craftsmen have a grievance against anybody, the courts are open and there are proconsuls. They can press charges. If there is anything further you want to bring up, it must be settled in a legal assembly. As it is, we are in danger of being charged with rioting because of what happened today. In that case we would not be able to account for this commotion, since there is no reason for it." After he had said this, he dismissed the assembly. (This was the case that ended up taking Paul to Rome.)

As the Lord Jesus was dying on the execution stake, he had asked his disciple John to care for his mother. After the Lord's ascension, John lived in Ephesus where he cared for Jesus's mother, as he had promised. This worked out well because he was the youngest disciple and the only one who had not been martyred. He lived in Ephesus for many years, teaching about the Messiah.

One of his premier students was Polycarp, who became a first/second century Christian apologist (among others such as Origen, Ignatius, and Irenaeus)—some say he was the first bishop—whose writings are an important link in the history of Christianity.

Others may disagree, but I believe literary evidence demonstrates that John was exiled to Patmos before he became an old man. The fact that he was not martyred was not his fault; according to church tradition and Foxe's *Book of Martyrs* (whose accuracy has never been discredited), the Romans made an unsuccessful attempt to kill him by boiling him in oil. There's certainly nothing shocking about the method, but what is shocking is that he didn't die. It's totally reasonable to assume they sent him straight to exile on Patmos from there. His stay on the island lasted two years, and during that time, he received and wrote the book of Revelation.

After returning to Ephesus, John continued to teach and care for Mary; during this time, he wrote the three letters. Some scholars believe that he wrote his gospel toward the end of his life because his disciples were urging him to get it done before he died. In any case, the influence of the *Revelation* is clearly discernible in John's other writings, indicating that it was written first. The *Gospel of John* is different from the other gospels because John had seen the glorified Jesus Christ before he wrote it. Although the other apostles had seen and interacted with the resurrected Jesus, they had not experienced the glorified Lamb of God. John had been exposed to a much bigger picture than the others had. The vision also influenced the tone and the content of his letters.

After John's death, the battle for control of the fledgling church swung into high gear. Every generation has its smart, greedy, ambitious sharpsters. Long story short: Marcion (AD 110–160) won the day. He is credited with founding the all-Gentile church, a hideous perversion of the body of Christ that has crippled it ever since, and also with naming the "Old" and "New" Testaments, a small but significant anti-Semitic detail. His primary objective was to sever the church from all Jewish influence, in effect equipping it with a ball and chain disguised as superior knowledge. (You know, like what happened to Eve.)

God ordained three yearly feasts for the Hebrews: *Pesach*, Passover, the Feast of Unleavened Bread; *Shavuot*, the Feast of Weeks (Pentecost); and *Sukkot*, the Feast of Tabernacles. Each is a prophetic celebration of the Messiah and profoundly meaningful to Christian believers. Marcion pronounced these occasions heretical, even though at that time many believers were still worshipping in the synagogue as Jews. This has been an incalculable loss to the Christian church.

Marcion advocated making the church more accessible to pagans, scheduling Christian observations to coincide with pagan traditions. He is the one to thank for using Easter—even the pagan name—as the observance of the Resurrection, with colorful eggs and bunnies. He approved the use of fat babies with wings and tiny bows and arrows, changing their name from Cupid to cherub. The real cherubim, who have six wings and are covered with eyes, are evidently just too disturbing, right? And also, celebrating the birth in the stable at winter solstice was just convenient for everyone.

Conclusion: Satan's Haymaker and the Real Conspiracy

Three Jewish feasts were ordained by God, and God requires the Jews to observe them. God has never required anybody to celebrate Christmas or Easter.

As soon as it was humanly possible, Catholicism became a corporate endeavor managed by a bureaucratic hierarchy. The Council of Laodicea and the Council of Nicaea in the middle of the fourth century, along with other factors, solidified its structure and stabilized its influence for the long term. Catholicism has been successful establishing itself all over the world by immediately and expertly incorporating local traditions and beliefs into the liturgy of the local assembly. This is no better exemplified than at Ephesus. Shifting from the virgin goddess to the virgin mother of Jesus was easy, and the lucrative craft of making beautiful representations of the Virgin Mother of God, the Queen of Heaven, was not disrupted.

Polycarp said Marcion was the spawn of the devil.

During the third century AD, the living body of Christ had not yet become Catholic. Here is a true account from the website *EyeWitness to History,* "Death of a Martyr":

> *Vibia Perpetua was a young woman of noble birth. She was twenty-two, a wife, a mother of a young son and a Christian. In the city of Carthage in North Africa, on March 7 of the year 203, she was put to death for her religious convictions. Her story comes to us from three eyewitness accounts written shortly after her death.*
>
> *Perpetua was one of five Christians condemned to death in the arena. (One of her companions, Felicitas, was a slave and eight months pregnant. Two days before her execution she gave birth to a daughter.) Pepetua's father was a pagan and came often to the prison (many times with Perpetua's son in his arms) to plead with his daughter to renounce her religion and save her life—to no avail.*
>
> *On March 7, Perpetua and her four companions were led to the arena where the crowd*

demanded they be scourged. Then a boar, a bear, and a leopard were loosened upon the men, while the women were attacked by a wild bull. Wounded, Perpetua was then put to the sword.

"When I was in the hands of the persecutors, my father in his tender solicitude tried hardto pervert me from the faith. 'My father,' I said, 'you see this pitcher. Can we call it by any other name than what it is?'

'No,' he said.

'Nor can I' [I said], 'call myself by any other name than that of Christian.' So he went away, but, on the rumor that we were to be tried, wasted away with anxiety.

'Daughter" he said, 'have pity on my gray hairs; have pity on thy father. Do not give me over to disgrace. Behold thy brothers, thy mother, and thy aunt: behold thy child who cannot live without thee. Do not destroy us all.' Thus spake my father, kissing my hands, and throwing himself at my feet. And I wept because of my father, for he alone of all my family would not rejoice in my martyrdom. So I comforted him, saying: 'In this trial what God determines will take place. We are not in our own keeping, but in God's.' So he left me—weeping bitterly.

[Perpetua and another Christian woman, Felicitas, were tossed and gored by a bull; but despite cruel manglings yet survived. Perpetua, says a sympathizing recorder] seemed in a trance. 'When are we to be tossed?' she asked, and could scarcely be induced to believe that she had suffered, in spite of the marks on her body. [They were presently stabbed to death by gladiators] after having exhorted the others to 'stand fast in the faith and love one another,' she guided to her own throat the uncertain hand of the young gladiator."

Conclusion: Satan's Haymaker and the Real Conspiracy

Believers who manifest the fruit of the Spirit are victorious sovereigns regardless of the circumstances (another spiritual paradox), never victimized, even while being martyred. Nero was infuriated when burning Christians alive could not make them stop singing because they were clearly demonstrating, rubbing his nose in, his own insignificance.

In Acts 17, during his discourse with the philosophers at the Areopagus, Paul quoted from *Phaenomena,* an important poem written by the Greek philosopher and astronomer (<u>not astrologer</u>) Aratus at the end of the third century BC. The poem uses the original Hebrew/Arabic signs and designations for the constellations, which are credited (without disagreement) to Adam, Seth, and Enoch. Known as *Mazzaroth* in Hebrew and *zodiac* in Greek, it was virtually universal common knowledge among all ancient peoples.

Claudius Ptolemy, the "father of astrology," didn't invent horoscopes until about three centuries later, during the same era that Catholicism was established as a religion. A famous quote from L. Ron Hubbard, the creator of scientology, is "If you want to get rich, invent a religion," which is, of course, what he himself did. Claudius Ptolemy did the same, adapting and renaming the original constellations recorded in *Phaenomena* to correlate with pagan mythology. He also originated the concept of horoscopes, effectively changing the focus from "the gospel in the sky" to individual fortune-telling. Astrologers today cite Ptolemy's *Almagest* as the "ancient" source for their practice, but it can't compete with the anciency of Adam, Seth, and Enoch. (Much more info elsewhere.)

More than 1,500 years later, in the nineteenth century, another ancient planisphere was discovered inside the sphinx (Denderah), which agreed with *Phaenomena.* So actually, the *Almagest* is the least ancient source available and is itself a deliberate departure from the earlier sources.

Ever since Martin Luther heroically challenged the monolithic Catholic structure, official Christianity has exhibited a particular method of growth. The first stage is a revelation taught by a charismatic individual, which is quite possibly a valid insight. Then, sincere believers collect and become a flock, an indication that a new denomination is taking root. As the flock grows, committees (probably not called committees) are established to accomplish certain tasks: write a document defining specific beliefs of the group, create guidelines for the acceptable behavior of members, establish policies for handling money, clarify expectations for leadership positions, and other issues.

Then conflict enters through various members, motivated, of course, by personal sin: competitions for leadership, disagreements about money, jealousy for various reasons or no reason at all. Dissatisfaction (well-founded or petty) among the flock prompts the design of a structure of operations, hoping to make everything less personal and less contentious. Who makes the decisions? Who decides who makes the decisions? Now it can be called a denomination, or even a religion. It doesn't have to be a very large flock for this to happen. The sin that instigated the conflict in the first place is ignored and never mentioned again. By now the original revelation, the life-changing insight that initially inspired the group, has been relegated to a motto in beautiful calligraphy at the center of the denomination website's front page. The group's influence is growing, though, and a committee is formed to investigate the benefits of colloborating with a similar group in the next state.

Some see a successful transition from sincere and enthusiastic, but sometimes unreliable, human persons, to a stable and reliable structure. The structure offers employment, from message takers to accountants, child care professionals, musicians, all the way to top level executives and professional fund-raisers. It is by everyone's account a huge asset to the community, which is wonderful. But it's not Christianity, and it won't introduce anyone to eternal life.

As a matter of fact, a "Christian church" like the above deceives people into believing that they have been "saved" and will not go to hell when they die, if there even is a hell. Sins among the membership, especially the clergy, are ignored as long as possible, until something bad is going to become public knowledge, and then it's taken behind closed doors and dealt with secretly. We're in a different dispensation from the first century church, right? And if things go public, we'll go

Conclusion: Satan's Haymaker and the Real Conspiracy

down, all our good works will cease, and lots of people will be hurt. Right?

In this enlightened age, it is far more offensive to call someone a liar than to actually tell a lie. Honest people are viewed as socially awkward. Our culturally accepted conversation is a deluge of falsehoods, directed by strict, but unspoken, rules of etiquette. Conspiracy theories about global issues run amuck, exacerbated by the instantaneous communication made possible by the internet.

> *Woe to those who call evil good and good evil, who put darkness for light and light for darkness, who put bitter for sweet and sweet for bitter. Woe to those who are wise in their own eyes and clever in their own sight.* (Isa. 5:20–21)

(I encourage you to read the whole chapter at your earliest convenience.)

A recent review of Margaret Atwood's novel *The Handmaid's Tale* described the setting as "Christian totalitarianism." *Argh!* How has this happened in Western civilization, where biblical consensus has meant unprecedented prosperity to humankind? The word *Christian* has devolved into meaninglessness.

Sin brings judgment; it's a spiritual law, in the same way that gravity is a physical law. Some might call it karma. What goes around comes around. You reap what you sow. The wages of sin is death. God's holiness demands judgment; it's an equation that must balance. Frankly, I don't think demanding justice is in our best interest. We need to be pleading for mercy.

Our Creator loves us so much that He demeaned Himself horribly, not to confront the evils of the pagan Roman Empire (in which pedophilia, and other practices now deemed heinous, were commonly accepted facts of life) but to satisfy the judgment that each of us has earned through our own decisions and behavior. Jesus said, *"My kingdom is not of this world."* The Messiah did not come to condemn the world, but that the world through Him might be saved—eternally.

Christianity is not about social justice, which is, after all, only temporary. It's about eternal life. It's about becoming the infinite you, who you are meant to be: a child of God, joint-heir with Christ. Take a minute to wrap your imagination around that.

Roman civilization made a transition from socially approved paganism to socially approved Christianity within a couple of hundred years, the birth of what is now commonly known as Western civilization. No one burned any brothels or pagan temples. No elections took place. No public protests interrupted the daily life of the citizens. Nobody took up arms.

They did, however, go singing into the arena where they would be mauled by wild beasts.

Jesus paid it all. And, once again, God requires nothing from us but honesty, and He will even help us with that if we allow Him to. Accounting for the love of God fills gaps in academic attempts to explain human culture and civilization. No psychological, biological, or philosophical analysis can explicate that kind of love—love that enables victims to forgive their abusers, and heroes to sacrifice themselves for the good of others. Divine love—illogical, irrational, inexplicable—inspires the creation of music and art and dance that supersede human boundaries but are unknown outside the human species.

The Creator is worthy of worship, and worshipping Him fulfills the deepest needs of the human heart. The blood of the Lord Jesus Christ, the virgin-born Word of God made flesh, the prophesied Messiah, makes Him accessible to us. When we accept His truth and receive eternal life, we find ourselves relocated to an eternal reality that transcends, but includes, the universe we inhabit. (Being without the cocoon takes some getting used to.)

That is faith, "the evidence of things hoped for and the substance of things not seen."

> *I am executed with Christ, nevertheless I live, yet not I, but Christ lives in me, and the life which I*

> *now live in the flesh I live by faith in the son of God who loved me and gave Himself for me.* (Gal. 2:20)

And that eternal life, not subject to the universal laws of physics, is Light.

> *God is Light, and in Him is no darkness at all.* (1 John 1:5)

His works are continuously declaring His unchanging love for us, giving each of us as much of it as we can receive, whether we appreciate Him for it or not. We can't earn it. Even if we don't thank Him or recognize that it comes from Him, He still pours it out lavishly, because His love, as His vengeance, cannot be restrained.

He is calling you to come home. You probably already know you don't belong where you are. He knows that some will reject Him, but even so, He will continue to declare His love until the end of time. He is speaking. Let those who have ears to hear, hear.

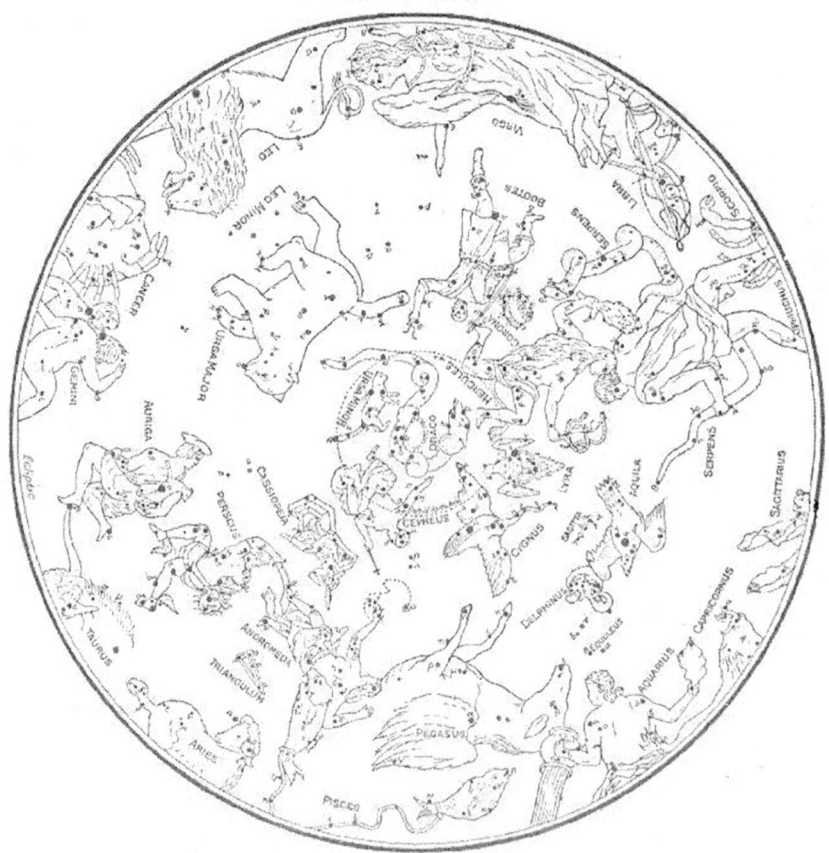

Chart is from Lost Constellation Testifies of Christ by John P. Pratt:
www.johnpratt.com/items/docs/lds/meridian/2004/prince.html

APPENDIX 1

Mazzaroth:
The Ancient Story in the Sky

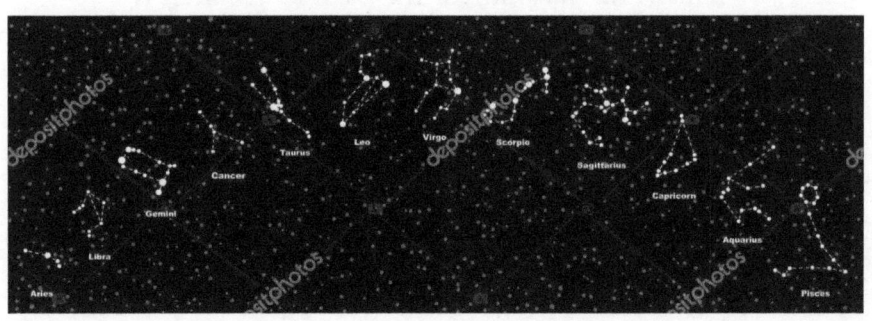

CHAPTER 1
The Christ

Sign 1: Virgo (the Virgin) ♍

The name of the constellation Virgo is based on the Arabic root *virgo*, which means "virgin." The maiden in the sky is always pictured holding a branch in her right hand and a sheaf of wheat in her left.

Stars: Spica, Arabic for "seed," and Al Zemach, Hebrew for "branch." Relevant Bible passages:

> Therefore the Lord himself will give you a sign: The virgin will conceive and give birth to a son, and will call him Immanuel. (Isa. 7:14)

> "And I will put enmity between you and the woman, And between your seed and her seed." (Gen. 3:15)

> "This is the meaning of the parable: the seed is the word of God." (Luke 8:11)

> A shoot will come up from the stump of Jesse; from his roots a Branch will bear fruit. (Isa. 11:1)

> "The days are coming," declares the Lord, "when I will raise up for David a righteous Branch, a King who will reign wisely and do what is just and right in the land." (Jer. 23:5)

> "Listen, High Priest Joshua, you and your associates seated before you, who are men symbolic of things to come: I am going to bring my servant, the Branch." (Zech. 3:8)

Decans of Virgo:

Centaurus

The Centaur is a mythological creature with a dual nature, part man, part horse.

Star: *Bezeh*, the Hebrew word for "despised." This mythical animal combination depicts the coming Savior, who is both God and man, and who would be despised. Many myths show evidence of being a muddled derivation of the original; for example, in Greek mythology, the centaur Chiron, a healer and prophet, chose to give up his immortality in order to save Prometheus from eternal suffering.

Relevant Bible passages:

> He was despised and rejected by mankind, a man of suffering, and familiar with pain. Like one from whom people hide their faces, he was despised, and we held him in low esteem. (Isa. 53:3)

Coma

A woman nursing a baby, called *Ihesu*, Hebrew for "desired one." Relevant Bible passages:

> 'I will shake all nations, and what is desired by all nations will come, and I will fill this house with glory,' says the Lord Almighty. (Hag. 2:7)

This constellation is no longer pictured as a woman nursing a baby, but is now called Berenice's Wig, for the wife of Ptolemy Soter III (246–221 BC), who was renowned for her gorgeous hair. She pledged that if her husband returned safely from battle, she would donate her hair to the gods, which she did. However, it was stolen from the temple where it had been displayed and disappeared, prompting her husband to claim that the gods had placed the beautiful tresses in the sky to honor her. Fortunately, the Roman word for hair (from which we get our word comb) sounds like the original name.

Bootes

A man striding forward (Egyptian *Smat*, "one who rules, subdues, and governs"; Hebrew *Bo*, "the Coming One")

Star: *Arcturus*, which means "the Coming One," and *Nekkar*, "the Pierced."

Relevant Bible passages:

> "Look, he is coming with the clouds, and every eye will see him, even those who pierced him; and all peoples on earth will mourn because of him. So shall it be! Amen." (Rev. 1:7)

Virgo summary

The sign of Virgo and the associated decans reveal that a dual-natured ruler, the desire of all nations, will be born to a virgin but will be despised and pierced.

Sign 2: Libra (the Scales) ♎

The constellation name means "balance" or "pound," from the same root that gives us the word *equilibrium*.

Stars: *Zube-al-Kenubi*, "The Price Deficient"; *Zuben-al-Chemali*, "The Price that Covers"; and *Zuben Akrabi*, "The Price of the Conflict."

Relevant Bible passages:

> "You have been weighed on the scales and found wanting." (Dan. 5:27)

Decans of Libra:

Crux (Cross)

The Southern Cross (Hebrew *Adom*, "the Cutting Off")
Relevant Bible passages:

The Anointed One will be cut off. (Dan. 9:26)

Victima (Lupus)

The Victim (Hebrew *Asedah*, ("to be slain"; Arabic *Sura*, "the lamb"; Greek and Roman *Harpocrates*, "silent victim of justice")

Relevant Bible passages:

> He was oppressed and afflicted, yet he did not open his mouth; he was led like a lamb to the slaughter, and as a sheep before its shearers is silent, so he did not open his mouth. (Isa. 53:7–8)

> All inhabitants of the earth will worship the beast—all whose names have not been written in the Lamb's book of life, the Lamb who was slain from the creation of the world. (Rev. 13:8)

Corona (The Crown)

The Northern Crown (Arabic *Al Iclil*, "a jewel"; *Al Phecca*, "the shining")

Relevant Bible passages:

> But we do see Jesus, who was made lower than the angels for a little while, now crowned with glory and honor because he suffered death, so that by the grace of God he might taste death for everyone. (Heb. 2:9)

Libra summary

Libra and its decans present the scales of justice, the price of the balance being paid by a silent victim who suffers execution and receives a crown.

Sign 3: Scorpio (The Scorpion) ♏

(Arabic *Al Akrab*, "scorpion" or "conflict"; Coptic *Isidis*, "attack of the enemy")

Stars: *Antares*, Arabic for "the Wounding," and *Lesath*, Hebrew for "the Perverse"

Relevant Bible passages:

> They had tails with stingers, like scorpions, and in their tails they had power to torment people for five months. They had as king over them the angel of the Abyss, whose name in Hebrew is Abaddon and in Greek is Apollyon (Destroyer). (Rev. 9:10–11)

Decans of Scorpio:

Ophiucus (the Serpent-holder)

Greek *Aesculapius*—being stung by Scorpio on his left heel, but crushing the head of Scorpio with his right foot, while restraining Serpens.

Relevant Bible passages:

> So the Lord God said to the serpent... "I will put enmity between you and the woman, and between your offspring and hers; he will crush your head, and you will strike his heel." (Gen. 3:14–15)

Serpens (the Serpent)

Reaching for the crown, Corona; restrained by Ophiucus

Relevant Bible passages:

> How you have fallen from heaven, morning star, son of the dawn! You have been cast down to the earth, you who once laid low the nations! You

said in your heart, "I will ascend to the heavens; I
will raise my throne above the stars of God; I will
sit enthroned on the mount of assembly, on the
utmost heights of Mount Zaphon. I will ascend
above the tops of the clouds; I will make myself
like the Most High." (Isa. 14:12–14)

Hercules (the Mighty One)
Man kneeling with a raised club and holding the three-headed dog Cerberus, guardian of Hades; Hebrew *Gibbor*, "the Mighty One."
Star: Arabic *Ras-Al-Gethi*, "the Head of Him Who Bruises"
Relevant Bible passage:

I am the Living One; I was dead, and now look, I
am alive forever and ever! And I hold the keys of
death and Hades. (Rev. 1:18)

Scorpio summary

In Scorpio, our enemy, the destroyer known as the serpent, is reaching for the crown but being held back by a powerful hero who, although stung on the heel, conquers death and hell.

Sign 4: Sagittarius (The Archer) ♐

This sign is also a centaur (dual-natured, heaven-born), shown drawing a bow and aiming an arrow at Antares, the heart of the Scorpion.
Star: Hebrew *Naim*, "The Gracious One"
Relevant Bible passages:

In your majesty ride forth victoriously In the
cause of truth, humility and justice; let your right
hand achieve awesome deeds. Let your sharp
arrows pierce the hearts of the king's enemies; let

the nations fall beneath your feet. Your throne, O God, will last forever and ever; a scepter of justice will be the scepter of your kingdom. (Ps. 45:4–6)

I looked, and there before me was a white horse! Its rider held a bow, and he was given a crown, and he rode out as a conqueror bent on conquest. (Rev. 6:2)

Decans of Sagittarius:

Lyra (the Harp)
Pictured as an eagle rising with a harp; *lyra*, "praise for the conqueror"
Star: *Vega*, "He shall be exalted."
Relevant Bible passages:

> Then I will go to the altar of God, to God, my joy and my delight. I will praise you with the lyre, O God, my God. (Ps. 43:4)

> Awake, my soul! Awake, harp and lyre! I will awaken the dawn. (Ps. 57:8)

Ara (the Altar)
Always pictured upside down, pouring fire into *Tartarus* (outer darkness); *ara*, "consuming fire prepared for his enemies"
Relevant Bible passages:

> Your hand will lay hold on all your enemies; your right hand will seize your foes. When you appear for battle, you will burn them up as in a blazing furnace. The Lord will swallow them up in his wrath, and his fire will consume them. You will destroy their descendants from the earth, their posterity from mankind. Though they plot evil

against you and devise wicked schemes, they cannot succeed. You will make them turn their backs when you aim at them with drawn bow. Be exalted in your strength, Lord we will sing and praise your might. (Ps. 21:8–13)

Draco (the Dragon)

Its head is under the foot of Hercules; Greek *dracon*, "trodden down"

Stars: Hebrew *Thuban*, "the Subtle"; *Rastaban*, "the Head of the Subtle"; and *Ethanin*, "the Long Serpent" or "Dragon"

Relevant Bible passages:

> The great dragon was hurled down—that ancient serpent called the devil, or Satan, who leads the whole world astray. He was hurled to the earth, and his angels with him. Then I heard a loud voice in heaven say: "Now have come the salvation and the power and the kingdom of our God, and the authority of his Messiah. For the accuser of our brothers and sisters, who accuses them before our God day and night, has been hurled down." (Rev. 12:9–10)

Sagittarius summary

Sagittarius ends the first chapter of the celestial story on a joyful note with praise for the conquering hero, the dual-natured one, whose enemy the dragon is utterly defeated and doomed to consuming fire.

NOTE:

EACH OF THE THREE CHAPTERS IN THE HEAVENLY BOOK CONCLUDES WITH THE DEFEAT OF SATAN: THE DRAGON, THE SEA MONSTER, AND THE SERPENT.

CHAPTER 2
The Church

Sign 5: Capricorn (the sea-goat) ♑

This sign is another example of a mythical creature being used to depict a spiritual truth. The goat is pictured with its head down, a foreleg bent underneath as if falling in death; the fish-tail, on the other hand, is always shown twisting upward as if wriggling vigorously.

In Hebrew the sign is called *Gedi*, "kid"; Denderah *Hupenius*, "the place of the sacrifice."

Stars: *Deneb al Gedi*, "the judge cometh"; *Al Dhabi*, "the sacrifice slain"; *Al Dshabeh*, "the killing of the sacrifice"; *Ma'Asad*, "the slaying"; and *Sa'ad al Naschira*, "the record of the cutting off."

In the Bible, a goat denotes a sacrificial sin offering, and a fish is commonly recognized as a symbol for the church, the assembly of those who believe in Jesus, the Messiah. The Greek icythus "fish" is a well-known acronym for "Jesus Christ, Son of God, Savior." The living church, the body of Christ, is born out of the dying body of the sacrificial sin offering.

Relevant Bible passages:

> Aaron then brought the offering that was for the people. He took the goat for the people's sin offering and slaughtered it and offered it for a sin offering. (Lev. 9:15)

> "But now I will send for many fishermen," declares the Lord, "and they will catch them." (Jer. 16:16)

> As Jesus was walking beside the Sea of Galilee, he saw two brothers, Simon called Peter and his brother Andrew. They were casting a net into the lake, for they were fishermen. "Come, follow me," Jesus said, "and I will send you out to fish for

people." At once they left their nets and followed him. (Matt. 4:18–20)

Once again, the kingdom of heaven is like a net that was let down into the lake and caught all kinds of fish. (Matt. 13:47)

Decans of Capricorn:

Sagitta (The Arrow)
Pointed toward Aquila, the falling eagle
Stars: *kaos*, "the arrow" and Hebrew *Scham*, "destroying"
Relevant Bible passages:

> Lord, do not rebuke me in your anger or discipline me in your wrath. Your arrows have pierced me, and your hand has come down on me. (Ps. 38:1–2)

> He drew his bow and made me the target for his arrows. He pierced my heart with arrows from his quiver. (Lam. 3:12–13)

Aquila (the Eagle)
The falling eagle; *Denderah Su-At*, "He is coming"
Stars: Hebrew *Tarared*, "the wounded"; Arabic *Al Shain*, "the scarlet colored"; *Al Cair*, "the piercing"; *Al Okab*, "wounded in the heel." The correlation with the protoevangelium is clear.

Delphinus
A fish leaping upward (mirrors the tail of Capricorn)
Stars: Hebrew *Dalaph*, "water pouring out"; Arabic *Scalooin*, "coming quickly"; Chaldean *Rotaneb*, "swiftly running water"

Capricorn summary

Biblical symbols are consistent. Water denotes the Holy Spirit, the water of life; the fish denotes Christian believers, the church; the eagle is a type of Christ. The Christ will be pierced, wounded, and will fall, receiving the just punishment that men deserve, but will return quickly, bringing water—life, the Holy Spirit—to the church.

Sign 6: Aquarius (The Water-pourer) ♒

Hebrew *Deli*; Arabic, Syraic *Delu*, "Water Urn"; Coptic *Hupei Tyrion*, "the place of his coming down as rain"; Greek *Hydrokeous*, "the pourer forth of water"; Egyptian (Dendera) *Aru*, "the river"

Stars: Arabic *Sa'ad al Melik*, "the record of the pouring out"; Arabic *Saad al Suud*, "he who goes and returns"; Hebrew *Scheat*, "who goes and returns"; Latin *Ancha*, "the vessel of pouring water"; Latin *Situla*, "small urn for drawing water."

Relevant Bible passages:

> For I will pour water on the thirsty land, and streams on the dry ground; I will pour out my Spirit on your offspring, and my blessing on your descendants. They will spring up like grass in a meadow, like poplar trees by flowing streams. (Isa. 44:3–4)

> "How beautiful are your tents, Jacob, your dwelling places, Israel! Like valleys they spread out, like gardens beside a river, like aloes planted by the Lord, like cedars beside the waters. Water will flow from their buckets; their seed will have abundant water." (Num. 24:5–7)

> Let us acknowledge the Lord; let us press on to acknowledge him. As surely as the sun rises, he will appear; he will come to us like the winter

rains, like the spring rains that water the earth. (Hosea 6:3)

Be glad, people of Zion, rejoice in the Lord your God, for he has given you the autumn rains because he is faithful. He sends you abundant showers, both autumn and spring rains, as before…

And afterward, I will pour out my Spirit on all people. Your sons and daughters will prophesy, your old men will dream dreams, your young men will see visions. Even on my servants, both men and women, I will pour out my Spirit in those days. (Joel 2:23, 28–29)

Jesus answered her, "If you knew the gift of God and who it is that asks you for a drink, you would have asked him and he would have given you living water."

"Sir," the woman said, "you have nothing to draw with and the well is deep. Where can you get this living water? Are you greater than our father Jacob, who gave us the well and drank from it himself, as did also his sons and his livestock?"

Jesus answered, "Everyone who drinks this water will be thirsty again, but whoever drinks the water I give them will never thirst. Indeed, the water I give them will become in them a spring of water welling up to eternal life." (John 4:10–14)

He said to me: "It is done. I am the Alpha and the Omega, the Beginning and the End. To the thirsty I will give water without cost from the spring of the water of life. Those who are victorious will inherit all this, and I will be their God and they will be my children. (Rev. 21:6–7)

Then the angel showed me the river of the water of life, as clear as crystal, flowing from the throne of God and of the Lamb down the middle of the great street of the city. On each side of the river stood the tree of life, bearing twelve crops of fruit, yielding its fruit every month. And the leaves of the tree are for the healing of the nations. The Spirit and the bride say, "Come!" And let the one who hears say, "Come!" Let the one who is thirsty come; and let the one who wishes take the free gift of the water of life. (Rev. 22:1–2, 17)

Decans of Aquarius:

Piscis Australis (The Southern Fish)

The stream poured out from Aquarius is flowing directly into the mouth of the Southern Fish; Denderah *Aar,* "a stream." Biblical symbols are consistent; this sign depicts the church receiving the poured out Holy Spirit.

Star: Arabic *Fom al Haut,* "The mouth of the fish"

Pegasus (Winged Horse)

This sign portrays only the front half of a winged horse, name from the Hebrew *Pega* "chief"; *Sus* "horse"; in Greek, Latin, "coming quickly, joyfully."

Stars: Hebrew *Markab,* "returning from afar"; Arabic *Al Genib,* "who carries"; Hebrew *Enif,* "the branch"; Arabic *Homan,* "the great king"; Arabic *Matar,* "to cause to overflow"; and Arabic *Biham,* "flock of kids or lambs".

Cygnus (the Swan)

Greek *cygnos,* "the swan circling"; Latin *cygnus,* "who comes and goes (or, circles)"; Denderah *Tes Ark,* "the one from afar."

Stars: Hebrew *Deneb*, "the Lord (or judge) comes"; also known as *Adige*, "flying swiftly"; Arabic *al Bireo*, "flying swiftly"; Hebrew *Sadr*, "who returns, as in a circle"; Hebrew *Azel*, "who goes and returns quickly"; Hebrew *Fafage*, "the glorious shining forth"; Hebrew *Arided*, "He shall come down"

Relevant Bible Passages:

> Listen! Your watchmen lift up their voices; together they shout for joy! When the Lord returns to Zion, they will see it with their own eyes. Burst into songs of joy together, you ruins of Jerusalem for the Lord has comforted his people, he has redeemed Jerusalem. (Isa. 52:8–9)

> "Therefore this is what the Lord says: 'I will return to Jerusalem with mercy, and there my house will be rebuilt.'" (Zech. 1:16)

> The evening meal was in progress, and the devil had already prompted Judas, the son of Simon Iscariot, to betray Jesus. Jesus knew that the Father had put all things under his power, and that he had come from God and was returning to God; so he got up from the meal, took off his outer clothing, and wrapped a towel around his waist. (John 13:2–4)

> "Do not let your hearts be troubled. You believe in God; believe also in me. My Father's house has many rooms; if that were not so, would I have told you that I am going there to prepare a place for you? And if I go and prepare a place for you, I will come back and take you to be with me that you also may be where I am. (John 14:1–3)

Aquarius summary

Aquarius portrays the outpouring of the Holy Spirit, bringing the water of life to the church, and emphasizes the promise of the Messiah's—here refered to again as the Branch—swift and glorious return to take His people home.

Sign 7: Pisces (The Fishes) ♓

Each of the two fishes in this constellation is about half the size of Pisces Australis; one swims along the ecliptic, the Sun's path, toward Aquarius, and the smaller faces due north, overlapping Andromeda, "the chained woman"; Hebrew *Dagin*, "fishes" or "mutitude"; Syriac *Nuno*, "fish lengthened out" (as in posterity); Latin *Pisces*, "fish" or also "multiplying"; Coptic *Pi-Cot-Orion*, "congregation" or "company of him that cometh"; Denderah *Piscis Hori*, "the fish of him who is coming." The two fish are believed by many to represent the Jewish people and the Gentile Christians.

Stars: Hebrew Okda, "the united," and Arabic Al Samaca, "the upheld"

Decans of Pisces:

The Band

The band attaches the two fish to each other by their tails and is also attached to the head of Cetus, the sea monster; the fish are in bondage to the enemy, which is sin and death. However, the figure of Aries (the lamb or ram), rests just over the head of Cetus, (the sea monster, depicting the law) and its foreleg intersects the band; Arabic *Al Risha*, "the band" or "bridle"; Denderah *U-or*, "He who is coming."

Relevant Bible passages:

> We know that the law is spiritual; but I am unspiritual, sold as a slave to sin. I do not understand what I do. For what I want to do I

do not do, but what I hate I do. And if I do what I do not want to do, I agree that the law is good. As it is, it is no longer I myself who do it, but it is sin living in me. For I know that good itself does not dwell in me, that is, in my sinful nature. For I have the desire to do what is good, but I cannot carry it out. For I do not do the good I want to do, but the evil I do not want to do-this I keep on doing. Now if I do what I do not want to do, it is no longer I who do it, but it is sin living in me that does it. So I find this law at work: Although I want to do good, evil is right there with me. For in my inner being I delight in God's law; but I see another law at work in me, waging war against the law of my mind and making me a prisoner of the law of sin at work within me. What a wretched man I am! Who will rescue me from this body that is subject to death? Thanks be to God, who delivers me through Jesus Christ our Lord! So then, I myself in my mind am a slave to God's law, but in my sinful nature a slave to the law of sin. (Rom. 7:14–25)

For the creation was subjected to frustration, not by its own choice, but by the will of the one who subjected it, in hope that the creation itself will be liberated from its bondage to decay and brought into the freedom and glory of the children of God. (Rom. 8:20–21)

So also, when we were underage, we were in slavery under the elemental spiritual forces of the world. But when the set time had fully come, God sent his Son, born of a woman, born under the law, to redeem those under the law, that we might receive adoption to sonship. (Gal. 4:3–5)

> It is for freedom that Christ has set us free. Stand firm, then, and do not let yourselves be burdened again by a yoke of slavery. (Gal. 5:1)

Andromeda (The Chained Woman)

Hebrew *Sirra*, "the chained"; *Persea,* "the stretched out"; Greek *Andromeda*, "set free from death"; *Desma,* "the bound"

Stars: Arabic *Al Phiratz,* "the broken down"; Hebrew *Mirach,* "the weak"; Arabic *Al Maach,* "the struck down"; *Al Mara,* "the afflicted"; Hebrew *Adhil,* "the afflicted"; *Mizar,* "the bound"; Arabic *Al Mosealah,* "delivered from the grave"

Relevant Bible passages:

> Shake yourself from the dust, arise; Sit down, O Jerusalem! Loose yourself from the bonds of your neck, O captive daughter of Zion! For thus says the Lord: "You have sold yourselves for nothing, And you shall be redeemed without money." (Isa. 52:2–3)

> "For your Maker is your husband, The Lord of hosts is His name; And your Redeemer is the Holy One of Israel; He is called the God of the whole earth. For the Lord has called you Like a woman forsaken and grieved in spirit, Like a youthful wife when you were refused," Says your God. "For a mere moment I have forsaken you, But with great mercies I will gather you. With a little wrath I hid My face from you for a moment; But with everlasting kindness I will have mercy on you," Says the Lord, your Redeemer…
> "O you afflicted one, Tossed with tempest, and not comforted, Behold, I will lay your stones with colorful gems, And lay your foundations with sapphires. (Isa. 54:6–11)

> The Spirit of the Lord God is upon Me, Because the Lord has anointed Me
>
> To preach good tidings to the poor; He has sent Me to heal the brokenhearted,
>
> To proclaim liberty to the captives, And the opening of the prison to those who are bound; To proclaim the acceptable year of the Lord, And the day of vengeance of our God;
>
> To comfort all who mourn,
>
> To console those who mourn in Zion,
>
> To give them beauty for ashes, The oil of joy for mourning,
>
> The garment of praise for the spirit of heaviness;
>
> That they may be called trees of righteousness,
>
> The planting of the Lord, that He may be glorified. (Isa. 61:1–3)

Cepheus (The King)

His right foot is on the pole star, so the heavens revolve around him. Hebrew *Cepheus,* "the branch"; Denderah *Per-ku-hor,* "this one comes to rule"; Ethopian *Hyk,* "the king."

Stars: Arabic *Al Diramin,* "quickly returning"; *Al Phirk,* "the redeemer"; *Al Rai,* "he who bruises or breaks" or "shepherd"; *Al Durab,* "returning in a circle."

Relevant Bible passages:

> The voice of the Lord breaks the cedars, Yes, the Lord splinters the cedars of Lebanon. (Ps. 29:5)

> He will bring justice to the poor of the people; He will save the children of the needy, And will break in pieces the oppressor. (Ps. 72:4)

> Therefore this iniquity shall be to you Like a breach ready to fall,

A bulge in a high wall, Whose breaking comes suddenly, in an instant.

And He shall break it like the breaking of the potter's vessel,

Which is broken in pieces; He shall not spare. (Isa. 30:13–14)

I will go before you and make the crooked places straight; I will break in pieces the gates of bronze and cut the bars of iron. (Isa. 45:2)

"Thus says the Lord of hosts: 'Even so I will break this people and this city, as one breaks a potter's vessel, which cannot be made whole again; and they shall bury them in Tophet till there is no place to bury.'" (Jer. 19:11)

The Portion of Jacob is not like them, For He is the Maker of all things; And Israel is the tribe of His inheritance. The Lord of hosts is His name.

"You are My battle-ax and weapons of war: For with you I will break the nation in pieces;

With you I will destroy kingdoms; With you I will break in pieces the horse and its rider; With you I will break in pieces the chariot and its rider; With you also I will break in pieces man and woman; With you I will break in pieces old and young; With you I will break in pieces the young man and the maiden; With you also I will break in pieces the shepherd and his flock; With you I will break in pieces the farmer and his yoke of oxen; And with you I will break in pieces governors and rulers. (Jer. 51:19–23)

So I will break down the wall you have plastered with untempered mortar, and bring it down to the ground, so that its foundation will be uncovered; it will fall, and you shall be consumed in the midst of it. Then you shall know that I am the Lord. (Ezek. 13:14)

Pisces summary

Fish must live in water to survive, as the church must remain filled with the Holy Spirit; deliverance from bondage to sin is not yet fully accomplished in the growing congregation; the King, the Redeemer, is again called the Branch, and his quick return is again emphasized, along with His judgment that breaks anything in its path. The chained woman, a type of the church, the bride of Christ, awaits deliverance.

Sign 8: Aries (The Lamb or Ram) ♈

The lamb is depicted resting, with one foreleg placed on the band connecting the fishes in Pisces, holding the reins of his people and restraining Cetus, the sea monster. In Hebrew *Taleh*, "the lamb sent forth"; Arabic *Al Hamal*, "the sheep gentle and merciful"; Coptic *Tametouris Ammon*, "the dominion or government established"; Akkadian Baraziggar, "the altar of the sacrifice for righteousness."

Stars: Arabic *El Natik*, "the wounded" or "the slain"; Arabic *El Sharatan*, "the bruised"; Hebrew *Mesartim*, "the bound." The earliest star charts place a triangle over the head of Aries, known in Hebrew as *Salisha*, "the exalted," and in Arabic *Deltoton*, "lifted up."

Relevant Bible passages:

> I drew them with gentle cords, with bands of love, And I was to them as those who take the yoke from their neck. (Hosea 11:4)

> And I looked, and behold, in the midst of the throne and of the four living creatures, and in the midst of the elders, stood a Lamb as though

it had been slain, having seven horns and seven eyes, which are the seven Spirits of God sent out into all the earth. Then He came and took the scroll out of the right hand of Him who sat on the throne. Now when He had taken the scroll, the four living creatures and the twenty-four elders fell down before the Lamb, each having a harp, and golden bowls full of incense, which are the prayers of the saints. And they sang a new song, saying:

"You are worthy to take the scroll, And to open its seals; For You were slain, And have redeemed us to God by Your blood Out of every tribe and tongue and people and nation, And have made us kings and priests to our God;

And we shall reign on the earth."

Then I looked, and I heard the voice of many angels around the throne, the living creatures, and the elders; and the number of them was ten thousand times ten thousand, and thousands of thousands, saying with a loud voice:

"Worthy is the Lamb who was slain

To receive power and riches and wisdom,

And strength and honor and glory and blessing!"

And every creature which is in heaven and on the earth and under the earth and such as are in the sea, and all that are in them, I heard saying:

"Blessing and honor and glory and power

Be to Him who sits on the throne,

And to the Lamb, forever and ever!"

Then the four living creatures said, "Amen!" And the twenty-four elders fell down and worshiped Him who lives forever and ever. (Rev. 5)

Decans of Aries:

Cassiopeia (The Enthroned Woman)

In direct contrast to Andromeda, the Chained Woman; always pictured holding a branch in one hand and dressing her hair or arranging her garments with the other; Cepheus, the King, is reaching out toward her with the scepter in his right hand. In Hebrew *Yofee*, "the beautiful"; Arabic *Dat al Cursa*, "the queen enthroned"; Denderah *Set*, "the daughter of splendor, enthroned."

Stars: Hebrew *Shedar*, "the freed" and *Caph*, "the branch."

The stars of the constellation Cassiopeia never set; they are always visible.

Relevant Bible passages:

> And I heard, as it were, the voice of a great multitude, as the sound of many waters and as the sound of mighty thunderings, saying, "Alleluia! For the Lord God Omnipotent reigns! Let us be glad and rejoice and give Him glory, for the marriage of the Lamb has come, and His wife has made herself ready." And to her it was granted to be arrayed in fine linen, clean and bright, for the fine linen is the righteous acts of the saints. (Rev. 19:6–8)

Cetus (the Whale)

The Whale or sea monster; the band of Pisces is attached to his head and held by the foreleg of the Ram; Denderah *Knem*, "the subdued."

Stars: Hebrew Menkar, "the chained enemy"; Hebrew *Diphda*, "the overthrown"; also *Deneb Kaitos*, "the judge of Cetus"; Arabic *Beten Kaitos*, "from the belly of the whale"; and Hebrew *Mira*, "the rebel"

Relevant Bible passages:

> Then some of the scribes and Pharisees answered, saying, "Teacher, we want to see a sign from You." But He answered and said to them, "An evil and adulterous generation seeks after a sign, and no sign will be given to it except the sign of the prophet Jonah. For as Jonah was three days and three nights in the belly of the great fish, so will the Son of Man be three days and three nights in the heart of the earth. (Matt. 12: 38–40)

> In that day the Lord with His severe sword, great and strong, Will punish Leviathan the fleeing serpent, Leviathan that twisted serpent; and He will slay the reptile that is in the sea. (Isa. 27:1)

> Then I saw an angel coming down from heaven, having the key to the bottomless pit and a great cchain in his hand. He laid hold of the dragon, that serpent of old, who is the Devil and Satan, and bound him for a thousand years. (Rev. 20:1–2)

Perseus (the Breaker)

Hebrew *Peretz,* "Breaker"; Persian *Bershaush,* "Breaker"; Denderah *Kar Knem,* "One who defeats Cetus"

Stars: Hebrew *Mirfak,* "He who helps"; Hebrew *Athik,* "He who breaks"; Arabic *Al Genib,* "He who carries away"; the trophy in the hand of Perseus: Hebrew *Medusa,* "the trodden underfoot"; Hebrew *Rosh Satan,* "the head of the adversary, Satan"; Arabic *Al Ghoul,* "Evil spirit" (now known as Algol)

Relevant Bible passages:

> "I will declare the decree: The Lord has said to Me, 'You are My Son, Today I have begotten

You. Ask of Me, and I will give You The nations for Your inheritance, And the ends of the earth for Your possession. You shall break them with a rod of iron; You shall dash them to pieces like a potter's vessel.'" (Ps. 2:7–9)

He breaks me with wound upon wound; He runs at me like a warrior. (Job 16:14)

How long will you torment my soul, And break me in pieces with words? (Job 19:2)

He breaks me down on every side, And I am gone; My hope He has uprooted like a tree. (Job 19:10)

That I will break the Assyrian in My land, And on My mountains tread him underfoot. Then his yoke shall be removed from them, And his burden removed from their shoulders. (Isa. 14:25)

Aries summary

This sign focuses on the lamb slain from the beginning of the world, who breaks the bondage of the oppressed, who crushes the adversary, and who releases the woman—the church, the bride of Christ—lifting her to a place of authority.

CHAPTER 3
The Consummation

Sign 9: Taurus (the Bull) (Rhinoceros) ♉

The forepart only of the charging bull is depicted; the rear is covered by Aries; Hebrew *Rhe'em*, "large fierce ox," "impossible to domesticate"; sometimes translated "aurochs" or "unicorn." This word, *rhe'em*, is translated in a variety of ways in different translations of the Bible. The word *unicorn* occurs in the King James Version, but the margin note reads "rhinoceros." The Revised Version consistently uses "wild-ox" with a margin note of "ox-antelope." The Septuagint uses *monokeros*, "one-horned," except in Isaiah 34:7, where the term *hoi hadroi*, "the large ones" or "the bulky ones" is used. The Vulgate uses "rhinoceros" and "unicorn." When and how the one-horned wild ox, impossible to tame, the rhinoceros became instead a common bull or a mythological one-horned horse is a mystery. Also known as Hebrew *Shur*, "the bull coming or ruling"; Arabic *Al Thaur*, "the bull coming"; Denderah *Isis*, "the one who saves mightily"; *Apis*, "the chief who comes"; *Horias*, "the traveler who comes to save"; *Statio Hori*, "the place of the one who comes to save."

Stars: Arabic *Al Debaran*, "the leader"; Arabic *El Nath*, "the slain"; Arabic *Al Cyon*, "the center"; Arabic *Pleiades*, Hebrew *Chima*, "the heap" (associated with doves); Syriac *Succoth*, "booths" or "tabernacles"; Hebrew *Hyades*, "the congregated"; Hebrew *Palilicum*, "belonging to the judge"; Arabic *Al Thuraiya*, "abundance"; Arabic *Wasat*, "the center" or "foundation"; Latin *Virgiliae*, "the center."

As Taurus rises in the sky, Scorpio sinks.

Relevant Bible passages:

> "God brings him out of Egypt; He has strength like a wild ox; He shall consume the nations, his enemies; He shall break their bones and pierce them with his arrows." (Num. 24:8)

"Will the wild ox be willing to serve you? Will he bed by your manger? Can you bind the wild ox in the furrow with ropes? Or will he plow the valleys behind you? Will you trust him because his strength is great? Or will you leave your labor to him? Will you trust him to bring home your grain, And gather it to your threshing floor?" (Job 39:9–12)

But You, Lord, are on high forevermore. For behold, Your enemies, O Lord, For behold, Your enemies shall perish; All the workers of iniquity shall be scattered. But my horn You have exalted like a wild ox; I have been anointed with fresh oil. My eye also has seen my desire on my enemies; My ears hear my desire on the wicked Who rise up against me. (Ps. 92:8–11.)

Therefore I will shake the heavens, And the earth will move out of her place,
    In the wrath of the Lord of hosts And in the day of His fierce anger.
    It shall be as the hunted gazelle, And as a sheep that no man takes up;
    Every man will turn to his own people, And everyone will flee to his own land.
    Everyone who is found will be thrust through, And everyone who is captured will fall by the sword. (Isa. 13:13–15)

Come near, you nations, to hear;
    And heed, you people!
    Let the earth hear, and all that is in it, The world and all things that come forth from it.
    For the indignation of the Lord is against all nations, And His fury against all their armies;

He has utterly destroyed them, He has given them over to the slaughter.

Also their slain shall be thrown out; Their stench shall rise from their corpses,

And the mountains shall be melted with their blood. All the host of heaven shall be dissolved,

And the heavens shall be rolled up like a scroll; All their host shall fall down

As the leaf falls from the vine, And as fruit falling from a fig tree.

"For My sword shall be bathed in heaven; Indeed it shall come down on Edom,

And on the people of My curse, for judgment. The sword of the Lord is filled with blood,

It is made overflowing with fatness, With the blood of lambs and goats,

With the fat of the kidneys of rams. For the Lord has a sacrifice in Bozrah,

And a great slaughter in the land of Edom. The wild oxen shall come down with them,

And the young bulls with the mighty bulls; Their land shall be soaked with blood,

And their dust saturated with fatness." For it is the day of the Lord's vengeance,

The year of recompense for the cause of Zion. (Isa. 34:1–8)

Decans of Taurus:

Orion (The Hunter)
Right hand raising a club; left hand lifting the severed head of a lion; the River Eridanus flows from a foot that is raised as if injured; Hebrew *Orion*, "one coming forth as light"; Akkadian *Ur-Ana*, "the light of Heaven"; Arabic *Al Giauza*, "the branch"; *Al Gebor*,

"the mighty"; *Al Mizam*, "the prince"; *Al Nagjed*, "the wounded"; Denderah *Ha-ga-T,* "this chief triumphs."

Stars: Hebrew *Betelgeuz*, "the coming of the branch"; Arabic *Regol*, "one treading underfoot"; Arabic *Belatrix*, "hastily coming"; Arabic *Mintaka*, "dividing the belt"; Arabic *Al Nitak*, "the wounded"; Arabic *Al Rai*, "the bruising"; Hebrew *Saiph*, "the bruised"; Chaldee *Hecke*, "the coming"; *Niphla*, "the mighty"; Hebrew *Meissa*, "the coming forth"; *Nux*, "the strong"; Arabic *Thabit*, "treading upon"; Hebrew *Kesil*, "bound together," "constellations," or "the burly, strong one."

Relevant Bible passages:

> "But who can endure the day of His coming? And who can stand when He appears? For He is like a refiner's fire And like launderers' soap." (Mal. 3:2)

> Be sober, be vigilant; because your adversary the devil, as a roaring lion, walketh about, seeking whom he may devour. (1 Pet. 5:8)

Eridanus (The River)

Issuing from the upraised foot, or heel, of Orion, and passing through the front paws of Cetus, the sea monster; (some planispheres show the River originating at Aquarius and winding its way through the Southern Fish to Orion) Hebrew *Eridanus*, "the river of the judge"; Denderah *Peh-Ta-T*, "the mouth of the river of water."

Stars: Hebrew *Phaet*, "the mouth of the river"; *Theemin*, "the water"; *Achernar*, "the after part of the river"; *Cursa*, "bent down"; *Ozha*, "the going forth"; Arabic *Zourak*, "flowing."

Relevant Bible passages:

> Then he brought me back to the door of the temple; and there was water, flowing from under the threshold of the temple toward the east, for the front of the temple faced east; the water was

flowing from under the right side of the temple, south of the altar... Again he measured one thousand, and it was a river that I could not cross; for the water was too deep, water in which one must swim, a river that could not be crossed. He said to me, "Son of man, have you seen this?" Then he brought me and returned me to the bank of the river. When I returned, there, along the bank of the river, were very many trees on one side and the other. Then he said to me: "This water flows toward the eastern region, goes down into the valley, and enters the sea. When it reaches the sea, its waters are healed. And it shall be that every living thing that moves, wherever the river goes, will live. There will be a very great multitude of fish, because these waters go there; for they will be healed, and everything will live wherever the river goes. (Ezek. 47)

I watched till thrones were put in place, And the Ancient of Days was seated; His garment was white as snow, And the hair of His head was like pure wool. His throne was a fiery flame, Its wheels a burning fire; fiery stream issued And came forth from before Him. A thousand thousands ministered to Him; Ten thousand times ten thousand stood before Him. The court was seated, And the books were opened. (Dan. 7:9–10)

Auriga (the Shepherd)

The Shepherd, holding a pair of reins (as the lamb does in the Band connecting Pisces), with a ewe and two lambs, one looking at Taurus, the other facing the Shepherd. This constellation was redesignated "the Charioteer" during the Roman era when other corruptions also occurred: Coma, the nursing baby, became Berenice's wig, and Gemini was changed from a man and woman walking side by side to the twins Castor and Pollux; Hebrew *Auriga,* "shepherd."

Stars: Hebrew *Alioth,* "the ewe" and Hebrew *Gedi,* "the kids"

Relevant Bible passages:

> He tends his flock like a shepherd: He gathers the lambs in his arms and carries them close to his heart; he gently leads those that have young. (Isa. 40:11)

> The Lord is my shepherd, I lack nothing. (Ps. 23:1)

> "I am the good shepherd; I know my sheep and my sheep know me just as the Father knows me and I know the Father and I lay down my life for the sheep. I have other sheep that are not of this sheep pen. I must bring them also. They too will listen to my voice, and there shall be one flock and one shepherd. The reason my Father loves me is that I lay down my life, only to take it up again. No one takes it from me, but I lay it down of my own accord. I have authority to lay it down and authority to take it up again. This command I received from my Father." (John 10:14–18)

> "Therefore, you shepherds, hear the word of the Lord: 'As I live,' says the Lord God, 'surely because My flock became a prey, and My flock became food for every beast of the field, because there was no shepherd, nor did My shepherds search for My flock, but the shepherds fed themselves and did not feed My flock'—therefore, O shepherds, hear the word of the Lord!
>
> Thus says the Lord God: 'Behold, I am against the shepherds, and I will require My

flock at their hand; I will cause them to cease feeding the sheep, and the shepherds shall feed themselves no more; for I will deliver My flock from their mouths, that they may no longer be food for them.'

For thus says the Lord God: 'Indeed I Myself will search for My sheep and seek them out. As a shepherd seeks out his flock on the day he is among his scattered sheep, so will I seek out My sheep and deliver them from all the places where they were scattered on a cloudy and dark day... I will feed My flock, and I will make them lie down,' says the Lord God. 'I will seek what was lost and bring back what was driven away, bind up the broken and strengthen what was sick; but I will destroy the fat and the strong, and feed them in judgment...and they shall know that I am the Lord when I have broken the bands of their yoke and delivered them from the hand of those who enslaved them...but they shall dwell safely, and no one shall make them afraid... Thus they shall know that I, the Lord their God, am with them, and they, the house of Israel, are My people... You are My flock, the flock of My pasture; you are men, and I am your God,' says the Lord God." (Ezek. 34:7–31)

Taurus summary

The charging bull (rhinoceros) signals the coming judgment on the enemy—Satan, the devil, the dragon, the serpent, the sea monster, the deceiver—of God and His people. The same river issuing from the wounded heel of the returning conquerer, the Branch, brings life to the church but fiery judgment to the enemy, as the conquering judge is to his people a gentle shepherd. How can the same River bring life to some and judgment to others? How can the same Lord be a charging rhinoceros toward some and a gentle Shepherd to others? (How can light be a particle and a wave?)

Sign 10: Gemini (The Twins) ♊

This sign was renamed Castor and Pollux, the twins, during the Roman era when other adaptations to the original zodiac were also made. Originally, this sign was pictured as a man and woman walking side by side, equal, at rest, and in peace. The Hebrew *Thaumin,* Coptic *Pi Mahi,* and Arabic *Al Taumin,* each mean "the united." As God created man as male and female to be one flesh, the returning Savior will be united with the church, His bride. The destiny of mankind, to be in eternal communion with the Creator, is realized with the defeat of the deceiver, and in the union of the Redeemer and the church.

Stars: Apollo, "the ruler"; Hercules, "the one who comes to labour or suffer"; *Al Hena,* "the hurt, wounded, or afflicted"; *Waset,* "set, established, or determined"; and *Mebsuta,* "treading under foot"; *Propus,* "the branch spreading"; *Al Giauza,* "palm branch"; *Al Dira,* "the seed."

Relevant Bible passages:

> That is why a man leaves his father and mother and is united to his wife, and they become one flesh. (Gen. 2:24)

> For this reason a man will leave his father and mother and be united to his wife, and the two will become one flesh. (Matt. 19:5)

> For if we have been united with him in a death like his, we will certainly also be united with him in a resurrection like his. (Rom. 6:5)

> But whoever is united with the Lord is one with him in spirit. (1 Cor. 6:17)

"For this reason a man will leave his father and mother and be united to his wife, and the two will become one flesh." (Eph. 5:31)

My goal is that they may be encouraged in heart and united in love, so that they may have the full riches of complete understanding, in order that they may know the mystery of God, namely, Christ, in whom are hidden all the treasures of wisdom and knowledge. (Col. 2:2)

In that day shall the Branch of Jehovah be beautiful and glorious; And the fruit of the earth shall be excellent and comely For them that are escaped of Israel. (Isa. 4:2)

"Behold, the days come, saith the LORD, That I will raise unto David a righteous Branch, And He shall reign as King and deal wisely, And shall execute judgment and justice in the land." (Jer. 23:5–6)

In those days, and at that time. Will I cause a Branch of Righteousness to grow up unto David; And He shall execute judgment and righteousness in the land. (Jer. 33:15)

You shall no longer be termed Forsaken, Nor shall your land any more be termed Desolate; But you shall be called Hephzibah, and your land Beulah; For the Lord delights in you, And your land shall be married. For as a young man marries a virgin, So shall your sons marry you; And as the bridegroom rejoices over the bride, So shall your God rejoice over you. (Isa. 62:4–5.)

> Behold, thou art fair, my beloved, yea, pleasant: also our bed is green. (Song of Sol. 1:16)
>
> *The term "my sister, my spouse" is used four times (Song 4:9–12; 5:1), indicating spiritual and marital union.*

> For your Maker is your husband, The Lord of hosts is His name;
> And your Redeemer is the Holy One of Israel; He is called the God of the whole earth. (Isa. 54:5)

> Beloved, now we are children of God; and it has not yet been revealed what we shall be, but we know that when He is revealed, we shall be like Him, for we shall see Him as He is. (1 John 3:2)

Decans of Gemini:

Lepus (The Hare)
Enemy; Denderah *Bashti-beki,* "confounded and failing."
Stars: Hebrew *Arnebo,* Arabic *Arnebeth,* "the enemy of Him that cometh"; *Nibal,* "the mad"; Arabic *Rakis,* "bound with a chain"; *Sugia,* "the deceiver."
Relevant Bible passages:

> Satan...will go out to deceive the nations in the four corners of the earth. (Rev. 20:7–8)

> I say this because many deceivers, who do not acknowledge Jesus Christ as coming in the flesh, have gone out into the world. Any such person is the deceiver and the antichrist. (2 John 1:7)

Canis Major (The Great Dog)

Denerah *Apes,* "the head" (pictured as a hawk, *Naz,* "caused to come forth, coming swiftly down"); Hebrew, Persian *Zeeb,* "a wolf."

Stars: *Sirius,* "the Prince" (the brightest star in the sky); *Tistrya* or *Tistar* (Sirius), "the chieftain of the East"; *Mirzam,* "the prince or ruler"; *Wesen,* "the bright, the shining"; *Adhara,* "the glorious"; Hebrew *Aschere,* "who shall come"; Arabic *Al Shira, Al Jemeniya,* "the Prince or chief of the right hand"; Egyptian *Seir,* "the Prince"; Hebrew *Abur,* Arabic *Al Habor,* "the mighty"; Arabic *Muliphen,* "the leader, the chief."

Canis Minor (The Lesser Dog)

Denderah *Sebak,* "conquering, victorious"

Stars: Arabic *Al Gomeisa* "the burdened, loaded, bearing for others"; Arabic *Al Shira* or *Al Shemeliya,* "the prince or chief of the left hand"; *Al Mirzam,* "the prince or ruler"; *Al Gomeyra,* "who completes or perfects"; *Procyon,* "Redeemer"

Relevant Bible passages:

> And all flesh shall know that I the LORD am thy Saviour, And thy REDEEMER—the Mighty One of Jacob. (Isa. 49:26.)

> When the enemy shall come in like a flood, The Spirit of the LORD shall lift up a standard against him, And the REDEEMER shall come to Zion. (Isa. 59:19–20)

> For I know that my Redeemer lives, And He shall stand at last on the earth. (Job 19:25)

> Let the words of my mouth and the meditation of my heart be acceptable in Your sight, O Lord, my strength and my Redeemer. (Ps. 19:14)

The term "Redeemer" is used more than thirty times in the Hebrew Scripture as a characteristic and name of the God of Israel.

Gemini summary

At the end of the age, the Redeemer (the one who has paid the debt) returns to take unto Himself His bride, the church, who is to walk side by side with Him in perfect union. He is the glorious ruler, the prince, who brings completion to all things.

Sign 11: Cancer (The Crab) ♋

The Denderah sign is *Scarabaeus,* symbolic of resurrection; but the name is *Klaria,* "the cattle-folds"; Arabic *Al Sartan,* Syriac *Sartano,* "who holds or binds"; Greek *Karkinos,* Latin *Cancer,* "holding or encircling"; Arabic *Khan,* "traveller's rest or inn"; *Ker* or *Cer,* "encircling"; Akkadian *Su-kul-na,* "the seizer or possessor of seed." The crab is, to the Jews, unclean; this sign signifies the inclusion of the Gentiles in the safety of the household of God.

Stars: Beehive cluster, *Praesepe* "a multitude, offspring"; *Tegmine,* "holding"; Hebrew and Arabic *Acubene,* "the sheltering or hiding-place"; Arabic *Ma'alaph,* "assembled thousands"; Arabic *Al Himarein,* "the kids or lambs"; *Asellus Boreas,* "the Northern Ass"; *Asellus Australis,* "the Southern Ass."

Relevant Bible passages:

> "Issachar is a strong ass, Couching down between the sheepfolds; and he saw a resting-place that it was good; And the land that it was pleasant; and he bowed his shoulder to bear, and became a servant under task work." (Gen. 49:14–15)

> About noon the following day as they were on their journey and approaching the city, Peter went up on the roof to pray. He became hungry and wanted something to eat, and while the meal was being prepared, he fell into a trance. He saw heaven opened and something like a large sheet being let down to earth by its four corners.

It contained all kinds of four-footed animals, as well as reptiles and birds. Then a voice told him, "Get up, Peter. Kill and eat."

"Surely not, Lord!" Peter replied. "I have never eaten anything impure or unclean."

The voice spoke to him a second time, "Do not call anything impure that God has made clean." This happened three times, and immediately the sheet was taken back to heaven. While Peter was wondering about the meaning of the vision, the men sent by Cornelius found out where Simon's house was and stopped at the gate. (Acts 10:9–17)

Remember your servants Abraham, Isaac and Israel, to whom you swore by your own self: "I will make your descendants as numerous as the stars in the sky and I will give your descendants all this land I promise." (Exod. 32:13)

Decans of Cancer:

Ursa Major (The Greater Bear)
Brightest star of the larger constellation: *Dubheh*, "a herd of animals"; Arabic *Dubah*, "cattle"; Hebrew *Dohver*, "a fold"; Hebrew *Dohveh*, "rest or security." (Hebrew *dohv*, Arabic *dub*, Persian, *deeb* and *dob,* mean "bear"; Hebrew *Dohver*, "a fold," and Arabic *Dubah*, "cattle," might easily have been mistaken by the Greeks and understood as "bear.")

Ursa Minor (The Lesser Bear)
Stars: Arabic *Al Ruccaba*, "the turned or ridden on," the Polar or central star; Greek *Cynosure*, "high in rising" that is, in heavenly position; *Kochab*, "awaiting Him who is coming"; Arabic *Al Pherdadain*, "the calves" or "the young"; the redeemed assembly; *Al*

Gedi, "the kid"; *Al Kaid,* "the assembled"; *Arcas,* or *Arctos,* "a travelling company" or "the stronghold of the saved"

Argo

The Ship; this constellation is no longer recognized; was always depicted as a ship backing into harbor, at rest.

Stars: *Canopus* or *Canobus,* "the possession of Him who is coming"; *Sephina,* "the multitude or abundance"; *Tureis,* "the possession"; *Asmidiska,* "the released who travel"; Arabic, *Soheil* "the desired"; *Subilon,* "the Branch"

Cancer summary

Cancer indicates the inclusion of the "unclean" in the multitudes of the family of God, accepted into rest and kept safe within the arms of the fold, at the end of the journey in safe harbor. Clearly, many images are repetitious and overlapping, including (but not limited to) the branch, the wounded, the pierced, the one who is coming, and the conquerer.

Sign 12: Leo (the Lion) ♌

Hebrew *Arieh,* "the Lion"; there are six Hebrew words for lion, and this one means hunting down his prey. Syriac *Aryo,* ""the rending lion"; Arabic *Al Asad,* "a lion coming vehemently, leaping forth as a flame."

Stars: *Cor Leonis,* "the heart of the Lion"; also known as *Regulus,* which means treading under foot; *Denebola,* "the Judge or Lord who cometh"; Arabic, *Al Giebha,* "the exaltation"; *Zosma,* "shining forth"; Hebrew *Sarcam,* "the joining"; Arabic *Minchir al Asad,* "the punishing or tearing of the Lion"; *Deneb Aleced,* "the judge cometh who seizes"; Arabic *Al Dafera,* "the enemy put down"

Relevant Bible passages:

The lion killed enough for his cubs and strangled the prey for his mate, filling his lairs with the kill and his dens with the prey. (Nah. 2:12)

The people rise like a lioness; they rouse themselves like a lion that does not rest till it devours its preyand drinks the blood of its victims. (Num. 23:24)

"Thy hand shall be on the neck of thine enemies; Judah is a lion's whelp; From the prey, my son, thou art gone up. He stooped down, he couched as a lion, And as an old lion; who shall rouse him up?" (Gen. 49:8–9)

"He shall eat up the nations his enemies, And shall break their bones, And pierce them through with his arrows, He couched, he lay down as a lion, And as a great lion; who shall stir him up?" (Num. 24:8–9)

Will a lion roar in the forest when he hath no prey? Will a young lion cry out of his den, if he hath taken nothing? The lion hath roared, who will not fear? (Amos 3:4, 8)

Then I saw in the right hand of him who sat on the throne a scroll with writing on both sides and sealed with seven seals. And I saw a mighty angel proclaiming in a loud voice, "Who is worthy to break the seals and open the scroll?" But no one in heaven or on earth or under the earth could open the scroll or even look inside it. I wept and wept because no one was found who was worthy to open the scroll or look inside. Then one of the elders said to me, "Do not weep! See, the Lion of the tribe of Judah, the Root of David, has triumphed. He is able to open the scroll and its seven seals." (Rev. 5:1–5)

Decans of Leo:

Hydra (The Serpent)
It means "He is abhorred."
Stars: Arabic *Al Phard*, "the separated, put away"; *Al Drian*, "the abhorred"; *Minchar al Sugia*, "the piercing of the deceiver"

Crater (The Cup)
Symbolic of wrath and judgment
Relevant Bible passages:

> God is the Judge. He putteth down one, and setteth
>   up another,
> For in the hand of the Lord there is a cup,
> And the wine is red; it is full of mixture,
> And He poureth out of the same:
> But the dregs thereof, all the wicked of the earth
> shall wring them out and drink them. (Ps. 75:8)

> Upon the wicked he shall rain snares, Fire and brimstone, and a horrible tempest: This shall be the portion of their cup. (Ps. 11:6)

> The cup of His indignation (Rev. 14:10)

> The cup of the wine of the fierceness of his wrath (Rev. 16:19)

Corvus (The Raven)
Denderah *Her-na*; *Her*, "enemy"; *Na*, "breaking up or failing"
Nine major stars: (the number of judgment): Arabic *Al Chibar*, "joining together"; Hebrew *Chiba*, "accursed"; Arabic *Al Goreb*, from

Hebrew *Oreb,* "raven"; Arabic *Minchar al Gorab,* "the raven tearing to pieces"

Relevant Bible passages:

> The eye that mocketh at his father, And despiseth to obey his mother, The ravens of the valley shall pick it out. (Prov. 30:17)

> When the great day of this judgment comes, an angel standing in the sun will cry to all the fowls that fly in the midst of heaven, Come, and gather yourselves together unto the supper of the great God; that ye may eat the flesh of kings, and the flesh of captains, and the flesh of mighty men, and the flesh of horses, and of them that sit on them, and the flesh of all men, both free and bond, both small and great. (Rev. 19:17–18)

Leo summary

Leo and its decans present an unadulterated picture of God's wrath and judgment at the end of the age. The people of God are safe and at rest, but His enemies are thoroughly destroyed and humiliated. Throughout the cycle of the constellations, metaphors, symbolic images, and star names are consistent with the biblical message of the coming Messiah bringing freedom from bondage, rest and fulfillment to His people and eternal judgment on His enemy, the deceiver, the devil.

APPENDIX 2

Transposition
C.S. Lewis

I. Transposition

A sermon preached on Whit-Sunday in Mansfield College Chapel, Oxford

In the church to which I belong, this day is set apart for commemorating the descent of the Holy Ghost upon the first Christians shortly after the Ascension. I want to consider one of the phenomena which accompanied, or followed, this descent; the phenomenon which our translation calls "speaking with tongues" and which the learned call glossolalia. You will not suppose that I think this the most important aspect of Pentecost, but I have two reasons for selecting it. In the first place it would be ridiculous for me to speak about the nature of the Holy Ghost or the modes of His operation: that would be an attempt to teach where I have nearly all to learn. In the second place, glossolalia has often been a stumbling-block to me. It is, to be frank, an embarrassing phenomenon. St. Paul himself seems to have been rather embarrassed by it in 1 Corinthians and labours to turn the desire and the attention of the Church to more obviously edifying gifts. But he goes no further. He throws in almost parenthetically the statement that he himself spoke with tongues more than anyone else, and he does not question the spiritual, or supernatural, source of the phenomenon.

The difficulty I feel is this. On the one hand, glossolalia has remained an intermittent "variety of religious experience" down to the present day. Every now and then we hear that in some revivalist meeting one or more of those present has burst into a torrent of what appears to be gibberish. The thing does not seem to be edifying, and all non-Christian opinion would regard it as a kind of hysteria, an involuntary discharge of nervous excitement. A good deal even of Christian opinion would explain most instances of it in exactly the same way; and I must confess that it would be very hard to believe that in all instances of it the Holy Ghost is operating. We suspect, even if we cannot be sure, that it is usually an affair of the nerves. That is one horn of the dilemma. On the other hand, we cannot as Christians shelve the story of Pentecost or deny that there, at any rate, the speaking with tongues was miraculous. For the men spoke not gibberish but languages unknown to them though known to other people present. And the whole event of which this makes part is built into the very fabric of the birth-story of the Church. It is this very event which the risen Lord had told the Church to wait for—almost in the last words He uttered before His ascension. It looks, therefore, as if we shall have to say that the very same phenomenon which is sometimes not only natural but even pathological is at other times (or at least at one other time) the organ of the Holy Ghost. And this seems at first very surprising and very open to attack. The sceptic will certainly seize this opportunity to talk to us about Occam's razor, to accuse us of multiplying hypotheses. If most instances of glossolalia are covered by hysteria, is it not (he will ask) extremely probable that that explanation covers the remaining instances too?

It is to this difficulty that I would gladly bring a little ease if I can. And I will begin by pointing out that it belongs to a class of difficulties. The closest parallel to it within that class is raised by the erotic language and imagery we find in the mystics. In them we find a whole range of expressions—and therefore possibly of emotions—with which we are quite familiar in another context and which, in that other context, have a clear natural significance. But in the mystical writings it is claimed that these elements have a different cause. And once more the sceptic will ask why the cause which we are content to accept for ninety-nine instances of such language should not be held to cover the hundredth too. The hypothesis that mysticism is an erotic phenomenon will seem to him immensely more probable than any other.

Put in its most general terms our problem is that of the obvious continuity between things which are admittedly natural and things which, it is claimed, are spiritual; the reappearance in what professes to be our supernatural life of all the same old elements which make up our natural life and (it would seem) of no others. If we have really been visited by a revelation from beyond Nature, is it not very strange that an Apocalypse can furnish heaven with nothing more than selections from terrestrial experience (crowns, thrones, and music), that devotion can find no language but that of human lovers, and that the rite whereby Christians enact a mystical union should turn out to be only the old, familiar act of eating and drinking? And you may add that the very same problem also breaks out on a lower level, not only between spiritual and natural but also between higher and lower levels of the natural life. Hence cynics very plausibly challenge our civilized conception of the difference between love and lust by pointing out that when all is said and done they usually end in what is, physically, the same act. They similarly challenge the difference between justice and revenge on the ground that what finally happens to the criminal may be the same. And in all these cases, let us admit that the cynics and sceptics have a good prima facie case. The same acts do reappear in justice as well as in revenge: the consummation of humanized and conjugal love is physiologically the same as that of the merely biological lust; religious language and imagery, and probably religious emotion too, contains nothing that has not been borrowed from Nature.

Now it seems to me that the only way to refute the critic here is to show that the same prima facie case is equally plausible in some instance where we all know (not by faith or by logic, but empirically) that it is in fact false. Can we find an instance of higher and lower where the higher is within almost everyone's experience? I think we can. Consider the following quotation from Pepys's Diary:

With my wife to the King's House to see The Virgin Martyr, and it is mighty pleasant... But that which did please me beyond anything in the whole world was the wind musick when the angel comes down, which is so sweet that it ravished me and, indeed, in a word, did wrap up my soul so that it made me really sick, just as I have formerly been when in love with my wife...and makes me resolve to practise wind musick and to make my wife do the like. (Feb. 27, 1668.)

There are several points here that deserve attention. Firstly that the internal sensation accompanying intense aesthetic delight was indistinguishable from the sensation accompanying two other experiences, that of being in love and that of being, say, in a rough channel crossing. (2) That of these two other experiences one at least is the very reverse of pleasurable. No man enjoys nausea. (3) That Pepys was, nevertheless, anxious to have again the experience whose sensational accompaniment was identical with the very unpleasant accompaniments of sickness. That was why he decided to take up wind music.

Now it may be true that not many of us have fully shared Pepys's experience; but we have all experienced that sort of thing. For myself I find that if, during a moment of intense aesthetic rapture, one tries to turn round and catch by introspection what one is actually feeling, one can never lay one's hand on anything but a physical sensation. In my case it is a kind of kick or flutter in the diaphragm. Perhaps that is all Pepys meant by "really sick." But the important point is this: I find that this kick or flutter is exactly the same sensation which, in me, accompanies great and sudden anguish. Introspection can discover no difference at all between my neural response to very bad news and my neural response to the overture of The Magic Flute. If I were to judge simply by sensations I should come to the absurd conclusion that joy and anguish are the same thing, that what I most dread is the same with what I most desire. Introspection discovers nothing more or different in the one than in the other. And I expect that most of you, if you are in the habit of noticing such things, will report more or less the same.

Now let us take a step further. These sensations—Pepys's sickness and my flutter in the diaphragm—do not merely accompany very different experiences as an irrelevant or neutral addition. We may be quite sure that Pepys hated that sensation when it came in real sickness: and we know from his own words that he liked it when it came with wind music, for he took measures to make as sure as possible of getting it again. And I likewise love this internal flutter in one context and call it a pleasure and hate it in another and call it misery. It is not a mere sign of joy and anguish: it becomes what it signifies. When the joy thus flows over into the nerves that overflow is its consummation: when the anguish thus flows over that physical symptom is the crowning horror. The very same thing which makes the sweetest drop of all in the sweet cup also makes the bitterest drop in the bitter.

And here, I suggest, we have found what we are looking for. I take our emotional life to be "higher" than the life of our sensations—not, of course, morally higher, but richer, more varied, more subtle. And this is a higher level which nearly all of us know. And I believe that if anyone watches carefully the relation between his emotions and his sensations he will discover the following facts; (1) that the nerves do respond, and in a sense most adequately and exquisitely, to the emotions; (2) that their resources are far more limited, the possible variations of sense far fewer, than those of emotion; (3) and that the senses compensate for this by using the same sensation to express more than one emotion—even, as we have seen, to express opposite emotions.

Where we tend to go wrong is in assuming that if there is to be a correspondence between two systems it must be a one for one correspondence—that A in the one system must be represented by a in the other, and so on. But the correspondence between emotion and sensation turns out not to be of that sort. And there never could be correspondence of that sort where the one system was really richer than the other. If the richer system is to be represented in the poorer at all, this can only be by giving each element in the poorer system more than one meaning. The transposition of the richer into the poorer must, so to speak, be algebraical, not arithmetical. If you are to translate from a language which has a large vocabulary into a language that has a small vocabulary, then you must be allowed to use several words in more than one sense. If you are to write a language with twenty-two vowel sounds in an alphabet with only five vowel characters then you must be allowed to give each of those five characters more than one value. If you are making a piano version of a piece originally scored for an orchestra, then the same piano notes which represent flutes in one passage must also represent violins in another.

As the examples show we are all quite familiar with this kind of transposition or adaptation from a richer to a poorer medium. The most familiar example of all is the art of drawing. The problem here is to represent a three-dimensional world on a flat sheet of paper. The solution is perspective, and perspective means that we must give more than one value to a two-dimensional shape. Thus in a drawing of a cube we use an acute angle to represent what is a right angle in the real world. But elsewhere an acute angle on the paper may represent what was already an acute angle in the real world: for example, the point of a spear on the gable of a house. The very same shape which you must draw to give the illusion of a straight road receding from the spectator is also the shape you draw for a dunces' cap. As with the lines, so with the shading. Your brightest light in the picture is, in literal fact, only plain white paper: and this must do for the sun, or a lake in evening light, or snow, or human flesh.

I now make two comments on the instances of Transposition which are already before us:

(1) It is clear that in each case what is happening in the lower medium can be understood only if we know the higher medium. The instance where this knowledge is most commonly lacking is the

musical one. The piano version means one thing to the musician who knows the original orchestral score and another thing to the man who hears it simply as a piano piece. But the second man would be at an even greater disadvantage if he had never heard any instrument but a piano and even doubted the existence of other instruments. Even more, we understand pictures only because we know and inhabit the three-dimensional world. If we can imagine a creature who perceived only two dimensions and yet could somehow be aware of the lines as he crawled over them on the paper, we shall easily see how impossible it would be for him to understand. At first he might be prepared to accept on authority our assurance that there was a world in three dimensions. But when we pointed to the lines on the paper and tried to explain, say, that "This is a road," would he not reply that the shape which we were asking him to accept as a revelation of our mysterious other world was the very same shape which, on our own showing, elsewhere meant nothing but a triangle. And soon, I think, he would say, "You keep on telling me of this other world and its unimaginable shapes which you call solid. But isn't it very suspicious that all the shapes which you offer me as images or reflections of the solid ones turn out on inspection to be simply the old two-dimensional shapes of my own world as I have always known it? Is it not obvious that your vaunted other world, so far from being the archetype, is a dream which borrows all its elements from this one?"

(2) It is of some importance to notice that the word symbolism is not adequate in all cases to cover the relation between the higher medium and its transposition in the lower. It covers some cases perfectly, but not others. Thus the relation between speech and writing is one of symbolism. The written characters exist solely for the eye, the spoken words solely for the ear. There is complete discontinuity between them. They are not like one another, nor does the one cause the other to be. The one is simply a sign of the other and signifies it by a convention. But a picture is not related to the visible world in just that way. Pictures are part of the visible world themselves and represent it only by being part of it. Their visibility has the same source as its. The suns and lamps in pictures seem to shine only because real suns or lamps shine on them: that is, they seem to

shine a great deal because they really shine a little in reflecting their archetypes. The sunlight in a picture is therefore not related to real sunlight simply as written words are to spoken. It is a sign, but also something more than a sign: and only a sign because it is also more than a sign, because in it the thing signified is really in a certain mode present. If I had to name the relation I should call it not symbolical but sacramental. But in the case we started from—that of emotion and sensation—we are even further beyond mere symbolism. For there, as we have seen, the very same sensation does not merely accompany, nor merely signify, diverse and opposite emotions, but becomes part of them. The emotion descends bodily, as it were, into the sensation and digests, transforms, transubstantiates it, so that the same thrill along the nerves is delight or is agony.

I am not going to maintain that what I call Transposition is the only possible mode whereby a poorer medium can respond to a richer: but I claim that it is very hard to imagine any other. It is therefore, at the very least, not improbable that Transposition occurs whenever the higher reproduces itself in the lower. Thus, to digress for a moment, it seems to me very likely that the real relation between mind and body is one of Transposition. We are certain that, in this life at any rate, thought is intimately connected with the brain. The theory that thought therefore is merely a movement in the brain is, in my opinion, nonsense; for if so, that theory itself would be merely a movement, an event among atoms, which may have speed and direction but of which it would be meaningless to use the words "true" or "false." We are driven then to some kind of correspondence. But if we assume a one-for-one correspondence this means that we have to attribute an almost unbelievable complexity and variety of events to the brain. But I submit that a one-for-one relation is probably quite unnecessary. All our examples suggest that the brain can respond—in a sense, adequately and exquisitely correspond—to the seemingly infinite variety of consciousness without providing one single physical modification for each single modification of consciousness.

But that is a digression. Let us now return to our original question, about Spirit and Nature, God and Man. Our problem was that in what claims to be our spiritual life all the elements of our natural life recur: and, what is worse, it looks at first glance as if no other elements were present. We now see that if the spiritual is richer than the natural (as no one who believes in its existence would deny) then this is exactly what we should expect. And the sceptic's conclusion that the so-called spiritual is really derived from the natural, that it is a mirage or projection or imaginary extension of the natural, is also exactly what we should expect; for, as we have seen, this is the mistake which an observer who knew only the lower medium would be bound to make in every case of Transposition. The brutal man never can by analysis find anything but lust in love; the Flatlander never can find anything but flat shapes in a picture; physiology never can find anything in thought except twitchings of the grey matter. It is no good browbeating the critic who approaches a Transposition from below. On the evidence available to him his conclusion is the only one possible.

Everything is different when you approach the Transposition from above, as we all do in the case of emotion and sensation or of the three-dimensional world and pictures, and as the spiritual man does in the case we are considering. Those who spoke with tongues, as St. Paul did, can well understand how that holy phenomenon differed from the hysterical phenomenon—although be it remembered, they were in a sense exactly the same phenomenon, just as the very same sensation came to Pepys in love, in the enjoyment of music, and in sickness. Spiritual things are spiritually discerned. The spiritual man judges all things and is judged of none.

But who dares claim to be a spiritual man? In the full sense, none of us. And yet we are somehow aware that we approach from above, or from inside, at least some of those Transpositions which embody the Christian life in this world. With whatever sense of unworthiness, with whatever sense of audacity, we must affirm that we know a little of the higher system which is being transposed. In a way the claim we are making is not a very startling one. We are only claiming to know that our apparent devotion, whatever else it may have been, was not simply erotic, or that our apparent desire for Heaven, whatever else it may have been, was not simply a desire for longevity or jewelry or social splendours. Perhaps we have never really attained at all to what St. Paul would describe as spiritual life. But at the very least we know, in some dim and confused way, that we were trying to use natural acts and images and language with a new value, have at least desired a repentance which was not merely prudential and a love which was not self-centred. At the worst, we know enough of the spiritual to know that we have fallen short of it: as if the picture knew enough of the three-dimensional world to be aware that it was flat.

It is not only for humility's sake (that, of course) that we must emphasize the dimness of our knowledge. I suspect that, save by God's direct miracle, spiritual experience can never abide introspection. If even our emotions will not do so, (since the attempt to find out what we are now feeling yields nothing more than a physical sensation) much less will the operations of the Holy Ghost. The attempt to discover by introspective analysis our own spiritual condition is to me a horrible thing which reveals, at best, not the secrets of God's spirit and ours, but their transpositions in intellect, emotion and imagination, and which at worst may be the quickest road to presumption or despair.

With this my case, as the lawyers say, is complete. But I have just four points to add:

(1) I hope it is quite clear that the conception of Transposition, as I call it, is distinct from another conception often used for the same purpose—I mean the conception of development. The Developmentalist explains the continuity between things that claim to be spiritual and things that are certainly natural by saying that the one slowly turned into the other. I believe this view explains some facts, but I think it has been much overworked. At any rate it is not the theory I am putting forward. I am not saying that the natural act of eating after millions of years somehow blossoms into the Christian sacrament. I am saying that the Spiritual Reality, which existed before there were any creatures who ate, gives this natural act a new meaning, and more than a new meaning: makes it in a certain context to be a different thing. In a word, I think that real landscapes

enter into pictures, not that pictures will one day sprout out into real trees and grass.

(2) I have found it impossible, in thinking of what I call Transposition, not to ask myself whether it may help us to conceive the Incarnation. Of course if Transposition were merely a mode of symbolism it could give us no help at all in this matter: on the contrary, it would lead us wholly astray, back into a new kind of Docetism (or would it be only the old kind?) and away from the utterly historical and concrete reality which is the centre of all our hope, faith and love. But then, as I have pointed out, Transposition is not always symbolism. In varying degrees the lower reality can actually be drawn into the higher and become part of it. The sensation which accompanies joy becomes itself joy: we can hardly choose but say "incarnates joy." If this is so, then I venture to suggest, though with great doubt and in the most provisional way, that the concept of Transposition may have some contribution to make to the theology—or at least to the philosophy—of the Incarnation. For we are told in one of the creeds that the Incarnation worked "not by conversion of the Godhead into flesh, but by taking of the Manhood into God." And it seems to me that there is a real analogy between this and what I have called Transposition: that humanity, still remaining itself, is not merely counted as, but veritably drawn into, Deity, seems to me like what happens when a sensation (not in itself a pleasure) is drawn into the joy it accompanies. But I walk in mirabilibus supra me and submit all to the verdict of real theologians.

(3) I have tried to stress throughout the inevitableness of the error made about every transposition by one who approaches it from the lower medium only. The strength of such a critic lies in the words "merely" or "nothing but." He sees all the facts but not the meaning. Quite truly, therefore, he claims to have seen all the facts. There is nothing else there; except the meaning. He is therefore, as regards the matter in hand, in the position of an animal. You will have noticed that most dogs cannot understand pointing. You point to a bit of food on the floor: the dog, instead of looking at the floor, sniffs at your finger. A finger is a finger to him, and that is all. His world is all fact and no meaning. And in a period when

factual realism is dominant we shall find people deliberately inducing upon themselves this dog-like mind. A man who has experienced love from within will deliberately go about to inspect it analytically from outside and regard the results of this analysis as truer than his experience. The extreme limit of this self-blinding is seen in those who, like the rest of us, have consciousness, yet go about to study the human organism as if they did not know it was conscious. As long as this deliberate refusal to understand things from above, even where such understanding is possible, continues, it is idle to talk of any final victory over materialism. The critique of every experience from below, the voluntary ignoring of meaning and concentration on fact, will always have the same plausibility. There will always be evidence, and every month fresh evidence, to show that religion is only psychological, justice only self-protection, politics only economics, love only lust, and thought itself only cerebral biochemistry.

(4) Finally, I suggest that what has been said of Transposition throws a new light on the doctrine of the resurrection of the body. For in a sense Transposition can do anything. However great the difference between Spirit and Nature, between aesthetic joy and that flutter in the diaphragm, between reality and picture, yet the Transposition can be in its own way adequate. I said before that in your drawing you had only plain white paper for sun and cloud, snow, water, and human flesh. In one sense, how miserably inadequate! Yet in another, how perfect. If the shadows are properly done that patch of white paper will, in some curious way, be very like blazing sunshine: we shall almost feel cold while we look at the paper snow and almost warm our hands at the paper fire. May we not, by a reasonable analogy, suppose likewise that there is no experience of the spirit so transcendent and supernatural, no vision of Deity Himself so close and so far beyond all images and emotions, that to it also there cannot be an appropriate correspondence on the sensory level? Not by a new sense but by the incredible flooding of those very sensations we now have with a meaning, a transvaluation, of which we have here no faintest guess?

APPENDIX 3
Translation Clarification

Biblehub is an excellent online resource for quickly comparing various translations and paraphrases of Bible verses. Contemporary twenty-first-century paraphrases, as opposed to translations, can often be recognized by the attempt to omit or gloss over references to war, spiritual as well as physical. Allusions to heterosexual monogamy, such as husband/wife, bride/groom, and marriage, are also under attack, and it is these passages that are the backbone of the revelation of God's love and purpose for human beings.

ONE REALLY GOOD VERSE:
Jeremiah 15:16 (Biblehub)

- **New International Version**

    When your words came, I ate them; they were my joy and my heart's delight, for I bear your name, LORD God Almighty.

Translation Clarification

- **New Living Translation**

  When I discovered your words, I devoured them. They are my joy and my heart's delight, for I bear your name, O Lord God of Heaven's Armies.

- **English Standard Version**

  Your words were found, and I ate them, and your words became to me a joy and the delight of my heart, for I am called by your name, O Lord, God of hosts.

- **Berean Study Bible**

  Your words were found, and I ate them. Your words became my joy and my heart's delight. For I bear Your name, O Lord God of Hosts.

- **King James Bible**

  Thy words were found, and I did eat them; and thy word was unto me the joy and rejoicing of mine heart: for I am called by thy name, O Lord God of hosts.

- **New King James Version**

  Your words were found, and I ate them, And Your word was to me the joy and rejoicing of my heart; For I am called by Your name, O Lord God of hosts.

- **New American Standard Bible**

    Your words were found and I ate them, And Your words became a joy to me and the delight of my heart; For I have been called by Your name, LORD God of armies.

- **NASB 1995**

    Your words were found and I ate them, And Your words became for me a joy and the delight of my heart; For I have been called by Your name, O LORD God of hosts.

- **NASB 1977**

    Thy words were found and I ate them, And Thy words became for me a joy and the delight of my heart; For I have been called by Thy name, O LORD God of hosts.

- **Amplified Bible**

    Your words were found and I ate them, And Your words became a joy to me and the delight of my heart; For I have been called by Your name, O LORD God of hosts.

- **Christian Standard Bible**

    Your words were found, and I ate them. Your words became a delight to me and the joy of my heart, for I bear your name, LORD God of Armies.

Translation Clarification

- **Holman Christian Standard Bible**

  Your words were found, and I ate them. Your words became a delight to me and the joy of my heart, for I am called by Your name, Yahweh God of Hosts.

- **American Standard Version**

  Thy words were found, and I did eat them; and thy words were unto me a joy and the rejoicing of my heart: for I am called by thy name, O Jehovah, God of hosts.

- **Aramaic Bible in Plain English**

  And I have kept your commandments and I have done them, and your word was to me for the delight and for the joy of my heart, because your name is called upon me, Lord Jehovah God, The Mighty One.

- **Brenton Septuagint Translation**

  [Where's the subject of the sentence?] consume them; and thy word shall be to me for the joy and gladness of my heart: for thy name has been called upon me, O Lord Almighty.

- **Contemporary English Version**

  When you spoke to me, I was glad to obey, because I belong to you, the Lord All-Powerful.

This paraphrase is pared down and scraped clean, only barely communicating the immediate literal meaning, defrauding the reader of critical eternal significance. Remember, the reader is focusing on getting the passage into his consciousness; God will clarify it when He chooses, which will be the best possible time. This paraphrase doesn't even offer that option.

- **Douay-Rheims Bible**

    Thy words were found, and I did eat them, and thy word was to me a joy and gladness of my heart: for thy name is called upon me, O Lord God of hosts.

- **Good News Translation**

    You spoke to me, and I listened to every word. I belong to you, LORD God Almighty, and so your words filled my heart with joy and happiness.

This paraphrase is omitting allusions to war, which "God of Hosts"—God of Armies—is clearly an important detail. This is an example of deceiving people into thinking they know the gospel when they haven't really even heard it. Biblical references to bride and groom have also been "canceled," not only in the Bible itself but also in many denominational hymnals.

- **International Standard Version**

    Your words were found, and I consumed them. Your words were joy and my hearts delight, because I bear your name, LORD God of the Heavenly Armies.

- **JPS Tanakh 1917**

    Thy words were found, and I did eat them; And Thy words were unto me a joy and the rejoicing of my heart; Because Thy name was called on me, O LORD God of hosts.

- **Literal Standard Version**

    Your words have been found, and I eat them, And Your word is to me for a joy, And for the rejoicing of my heart, For Your Name is called on me, O YHWH, God of Hosts.

- **New American Bible**

    When I found your words, I devoured them; your words were my joy, the happiness of my heart, Because I bear your name, LORD, God of hosts.

- **New Revised Standard Version**

    Your words were found, and I ate them, and your words became to me a joy and the delight of my heart; for I am called by your name, O LORD, God of hosts.

- **NET Bible**

    As your words came to me I drank them in, and they filled my heart with joy and happiness because I belong to you.

"As your words came to me" suggests that the writer is passive, which is significantly different from "your words have been found," which suggests that the writer has been searching to apprehend God's Word. The reference to God's name has been entirely omitted.

- **New Heart English Bible**

  Your words were found, and I ate them; and your words were to me a joy and the rejoicing of my heart: for I am called by your name, Lord, God of hosts.

- **World English Bible**

  Your words were found, and I ate them; and your words were to me a joy and the rejoicing of my heart: for I am called by your name, Yahweh, God of Armies.

- **Young's Literal Translation**

  Thy words have been found, and I eat them, And Thy word is to me for a joy, And for the rejoicing of my heart, For Thy name is called on me, O Jehovah, God of Hosts.

This one is my favorite, solely because of the verb tenses used. Some of you grammarians will understand what I mean.

ABOUT THE AUTHOR

Bronwyn Randel, a retired high school English teacher, lives with her husband of more than forty years in the foothills of the Blue Ridge in northeast Georgia. During her years in the classroom, she continued her own education, culminating with an education doctorate in 2012.

Dr. Randel became fascinated with the Bible and ballet during childhood. She began studying the Bible seriously during her junior year in Stetson University. After graduation, she worked as a room attendant at the Duvall Home for Retarded Children (that was its name at the time) and learned to deeply cherish special-needs individuals. She met her husband while participating in a tightly-knit group of believers seeking God, quite a few of whom became newlyweds—including the Randels.

They later relocated to the Atlanta area where they began homeschooling their three children. Before moving to Southern Appalachia, she worked as an emergency medical dispatcher and also became part of a liturgical dance team, performing in various Christian assemblies in the area. Once settled in the mountains, the children, then teenagers, enrolled in the public high school, and Dr. Randel joined its faculty, spending the next eighteen years as a classroom teacher.

Along the way, both sons became Eagle Scouts and their daughter became a skilled horsewoman. The Randels helped found a community theater, the first in the area, which provided another welcome opportunity for dance and choreography. Dr. Randel is a respected Bible, as well as classroom, teacher in the community.

Printed in the USA
CPSIA information can be obtained
at www.ICGtesting.com
CBHW021616290624
10817CB00035B/218